Desmond King

YEMEN AND THE WESTERN WORLD

YEMEN
AND THE
WESTERN WORLD

BY

ERIC MACRO

LONDON
C. HURST & CO.

First published by C. Hurst & Company,
13 James Street, London W.C.2 in 1968
© ERIC MACRO

Printed in Great Britain by
Billing & Sons Limited, Guildford and London

ACKNOWLEDGEMENTS

I am indebted to the Council of the Royal Geographical Society for allowing me to use some material from my article 'The First Americans at Mocha' (*Geographical Journal*, Vol. 130, March 1964); the Editor of the Port of Aden Annual for some extracts from my 'The First British Embassy to the Yemen' (*Port of Aden Annual*, 1960–1); and the Council of the Royal Central Asian Society for parts of my 'Yemen, a Brief Survey' (*Royal Central Asian Journal*, Vol. 36, 1949), 'Leland Buxton in the Yemen, 1905' (*Royal Central Asian Journal*, Vol. 48, 1961) and 'The Yemen, Some Recent Literature' (*Royal Central Asian Journal*, Vol. 14, 1958). My thanks are also due to the Peabody Museum, Salem, Massachusetts, for permission to use Captain Luther Dana's sketch of Mocha on the cover.

PREFACE

The aim of this book is to provide those interested in the affairs of South-west Arabia with some historical background to the present political situation in the Yemen. I hope that I may be forgiven for narrating at such length the comings and goings of the various European trading voyages; my object here has been to show how the change came about in the eighteenth and nineteenth centuries between intense commercial activity on the one hand and political and military rivalry on the other. I have dealt in some detail with military operations during the last sixty years on the Aden–Yemen border. If the reader finds this tedious I can only say that, if nothing else, he has between the covers of the book a useful and probably unique chronicle of the events of those years. I must of course take full responsibility for any implied opinions expressed or any bias placed unwittingly on certain controversial questions, although I have tried to steer a middle course between extremes of interpretation.

It is still interesting to speculate which nation provided the first European to set foot in the Yemen. Modern research has served to dispel much of the doubt which surrounded Arnold von Harff's narrative of his journey there in the fifteenth century. We can only be certain that Ludovico de Varthema from Bologna travelled there in the first years of the sixteenth century and that the army of the Roman Aelius Gallus reached Marib a quarter of a century before the birth of Christ. However, for the purposes of this book it is not necessary to look at any European contact with the Yemen before the early Portuguese attempts to take Aden.

To add the customary list of those to whom I am indebted would, I have no doubt, appear as a pompous cascade of name-dropping. Let it be enough to say that I have worked with or received wise counsel from the greatest European names in Yemeni history and exploration, going back to those who knew the territory in the last century. At least, those still alive are spared the embarrassment of being mentioned here. This is more than can be said for my dear wife, conscripted by marriage nearly a quarter of a century ago into the unpaid posts of explorer, traveller, editor, critic, reader, librarian, research assistant and comforter in times of stress.

Siena, Ital   Eric Macro
June 1967

CONTENTS

INTRODUCTION

No historical study of a country's external relations can be under-
taken without an appreciation of its geographical environment
and its importance in its own right. The Yemen, occupying some
75,000 square miles of mountainous territory at the south-west
corner of the Arabian Peninsula, has perhaps, with the exception
of Muscat, had longer contact with the Western world than all the
rest of Arabia. This fact possibly follows a pattern of commercial
and hence political importance of tips, or heels and toes, of the
great peninsulas of the world. Arabia stands by itself in that both
its terrain and the fanaticism of its people have precluded any but
minor contact with the West, and that only at its extremities.
What then has been the position of the Yemen down the centuries
in relation to the rest of the world? It cannot claim any importance
in its own right; it has at present no workable mineral or other
natural resources of international interest and there are no
communications facilities which single it out as an international
highway or a port of call. Yemeni coffee, grown in the maritime
range, was fetched from Mocha in European ships for little more
than two hundred years and the port of Mocha was used for a
very short time at the beginning of the nineteenth century as a
coaling station for the new steamships plying between India and
Egypt.

Yet there has been constant intercourse with the West for the
past four or five hundred years. Therefore we must look elsewhere
to find reasons for the Yemen's importance to the West. Christian
outflanking of Islam and the birth of Western seaborne trade with
the Indies brought the first diminutive ocean-going ships from
Europe round the Cape into the Indian Ocean. Much later,
Europeans were able to shorten the route to the Indies by crossing
from the eastern Mediterranean shores to the heads of the Persian
Gulf and the Red Sea; later still the advent of the Suez Canal
determined the Red Sea as the through route from the
Mediterranean to India and the East Indies.

By the third quarter of the nineteenth century, the position of the Yemen in world affairs, such as it was, had progressed from providing an occasional haven for the early Portuguese seafarers to furnishing an export outlet for the coffee trade, a port of call and a trading entrepôt for Indian Ocean shipping, a coaling station for the early short-haul steamships and finally a coastal strip at the entrance to the Red Sea, the possession of which by a European power might embarrass a rival whose merchant, and indeed military, fleet would wish to make constant use of the Suez Canal. England's interest in the Yemen diminished when she found Aden to be a more adequate port for refuelling or revictualling. From Aden she was able later to exert a restraining influence on the aspirations of Italy and France on the Somali coast.

For almost a century and a half the Yemen was of importance to Great Britain because it lay on her route to India, once her communications through Egypt had become established. It took some forty years of meditation at the beginning of the nineteenth century for Great Britain to decide to take Aden; then from 1839 onward the Yemen became a thorn in the flesh of the Aden administration. Gradually a tenuous peace was made with the tribesmen surrounding the port of Aden until some sort of boundary between the Aden hinterland and the Yemen was established in the first years of the present century. In the next fifty years or so, Aden and the Yemen managed to co-exist through a series of small frontier skirmishes and the difficulties brought about by the Italian occupation of Abyssinia and the Second World War. It was not until after the death of the Imam Yahya in 1948 and the spread of Arab nationalism after the Second World War that Anglo–Yemeni difficulties ceased to be a matter for negotiation between Great Britain and the Yemen. The Russian cold war was carried to the Red Sea; Nasser had taken control of Egypt and was turning his attention to driving the British from where they remained in Arabia.

Aden meanwhile, for so long just one of a series of British military posts in the Indian ocean, had become for Britain a military base and bunkering port of the first importance. Hence, when her other imperial commitments were a thing of the past, Britain continued to confront the Yemen and its changing rulers in its old guise as an imperial power, right up to the late 1960s.

This towne of Moha is ye Chieftest towne of trade for Shipping in all Arabia Felix. It is scittuated about 15 Leagues within ye Straights of Babermandell in or neare ye Lattitude of D/13: M/23: wheare ye compafs varieth about D/12. M/30 West.

These quaint sentences open the legend, *A table of the moste Remarekable and principall places about Moha,* which Augustine Fitzhugh appended to his manuscript chart and panorama of Mocha in 1683. He was by no means the first European to describe this ancient Red Sea port. The charred and waterstained manuscript of the same region used and inscribed by Dom Joao de Castro in January 1541 can still be seen in the French official archives. Neither the English cartographer from Tower Hill in the city of London nor the Portuguese sailor, later to become Viceroy of India, could have envisaged that after the passage of three or four centuries 'the Chieftest towne of trade for Shipping in all Arabia Felix' would be converted from a rubble heap into a serviceable port by Communist Chinese coolies. Even those of us who still like to recall nostalgically the sultry Sana afternoons in the precincts of the al-Bakiliya mosque and the dusty evening walks out to the vines of Rhauda can scarcely, even now, come to realise the pace at which the world at large is shattering the slow and easygoing life of this mountain paradise of Arabia. Here in the Yemen, life and landscape are undergoing the most dynamic change in all the country's troubled history. But, as I have written in an earlier book, this Arabia Felix of Roman literature still holds its fascination. Even now, as the background to constant political upheavals, the green and fertile highlands still stand out as the barrier which ensured their centuries of persistent isolation. If Arabia is situated at the very crossroads of human destiny, the Yemen has certainly let the world pass her by – up to the time of Imam Yahya's death in 1948. Unscathed by the ebb and flow of the great empires of history which drove east from the Mediterranean or thundered westward across the plains of Asia, the Yemen developed her own exclusive way of life.

One of the last ancient south-west Arabian kingdoms was Himyar which, after a short Ethiopian occupation in the fourth century, was able to flourish until finally overthrown by a further wave of invading Ethiopians in AD 525. A Roman expedition setting out from Egypt in 24 BC under Aelius Gallus was all but swallowed up by the desert on its march southward into the Yemen. During the second Ethiopian occupation and a later period of Persian rule (AD 570 to 628) Christianity spread and was tolerated alongside Judaism. However, Badhan, the last Persian Viceroy in the Yemen, accepted Islam, and the new faith began to spread gradually through the length and breadth of the country. Opposition from the Ethiopian Christians prevented the rapid expansion of Islam until 631 when the Prophet Muhamad sent his son-in-law Ali to force the universal acceptance of the new faith upon the Yemen. On the death of Muhamad, the Caliph Abubakr succeeded him. Omar and Uthman followed and it was Ali who became the fourth Caliph after the murder of Uthman in 656. The question of Ali's succession to the Caliphate is one which has produced the two great creeds of Islam – Shiites and Sunnis. Sunnis are orthodox Muslims who consider that the first four Caliphs were elected on merit, not solely because of their family connection with the Prophet. Of the four schools of jurisprudence which subscribe to the Sunni creed the Shafei school is the one represented in the Yemen. Shiites recognise heredity as the major consideration in the election of the successors to the Prophet and they themselves are split into two factions: the Persian Shiites, who rate personal quality a determining factor in the election of Imams, or religious heads, and the Zeidis who require the election of Imams from descendants of the Prophet but place more importance on religious competence. No Shiite recognises the first three Caliphs of Islam, and the adherents of this creed in the Yemen are represented by the Zeidis – named after Zeid, a great grandson of Ali.

Zeid never went to the Yemen, and was killed in about 740 at Kufa in Iraq during a revolt in which he sided against the Caliph of the time. He became a religious and political martyr. By the end of the ninth century a considerable body of his adherents had become established in the Yemen alongside the orthodox Shafeis. Generally the Zeidis established themselves on the high plateaux of the Yemen, and in particular at Sada and Sana, whilst the Shafeis inhabited the southern lowlands and the coastal plains. The Yemen had, in the meantime, become a province of the Islamic Empire with the Caliphate centred on Baghdad and intermittent revolts against its overlordship continued throughout the seventh and eight centuries. The first Zeidi Imam, whose descendants, with insignificant exceptions, have ruled independent Yemen with varying success down to the present day, was al-Hadi Yahya, who in 893 founded the present Rassid dynasty. This line of successors takes its name from al Qasim ar Rassi, a sixth generation descendant of Fatima, Ali's wife and the Prophet's daughter.

During the first six centuries of their existence neither the Imams of the Zeidi persuasion nor those of the Rassid dynasty itself were ever able to subdue the whole of the Yemen; but the Rassids appear to have been remarkably persistent – finally emerging in 1919 as masters of the greater part of the territory. In the present context the internal upheavals in the Yemen up to the beginning of the nineteenth century are of little account.

The exploits of the Portuguese in the Red Sea and Indian Ocean at the beginning of the sixteenth century prompted the Mameluke Sultan of Egypt to invade the Yemen in 1514, but by 1517 the Ottoman Turks had, in their turn, occupied Egypt. In 1538 they captured Aden and soon afterwards installed a Turkish Pasha at Sana. This Turkish occupation of Yemen lasted barely a century but after that brief period of Ottoman dominion the Yemen was no longer to remain isolated from the outside world. The rise of the Ottoman Empire between 1326 and 1520 had set a great and impenetrable Infidel barrier across the overland route between Christian Europe and the East. The early enterprise of Prince Henry the Navigator enabled the Portuguese both to practise their crusading zeal and to pursue their quest for gold and spices; it helped them also to find the land of that legendary Eastern Christian ally whom they sought, Prester John.

Vasco da Gama's voyage to India in 1497, an outcome of Prince Henry's pioneering, had alarmed the Turks and was perhaps a contributory cause of the formation of the English East India Company over a century later. Having, up to that time, relied on receiving its Eastern goods from Venetian-controlled entrepôts in the Mediterranean, England was now in a position to seek the original sources of supply. The Hundred Years War with France had left her without the continental commitments upon which she had previously dissipated her resources; after the Wars of the Roses she was endowed with a centralised governmental system and an enterprising sovereign. Her population was increasing and home production of woollen cloth was already meeting the needs of the domestic market. The sea was her obvious outlet and, amply stocked with gold from the Spanish Main, she had reached the threshold of her greatest maritime enterprise. But as her early ventures round the Cape had revealed a great decline in Spanish sea power so did England begin to abandon her Mediterranean excursions in favour of the more lucrative, if more hazardous, long sea route to the East. The Crusades had reawakened an isolated Europe and an insular England to the amenities of a long forgotten Eastern civilisation, and silks became one of the principal Eastern commodities to be demanded by those who could afford them. The lack of winter feed for cattle called for advance slaughtering of animals for the winter months and spices were constantly and urgently in demand for preserving and seasoning meats. The capture of Constantinople by the Turks in 1453 finally put an end to the Venetian monopoly of supplying these Eastern goods to Europe; and it also had stimulated the search for the alternative route via the Cape to the Eastern markets.

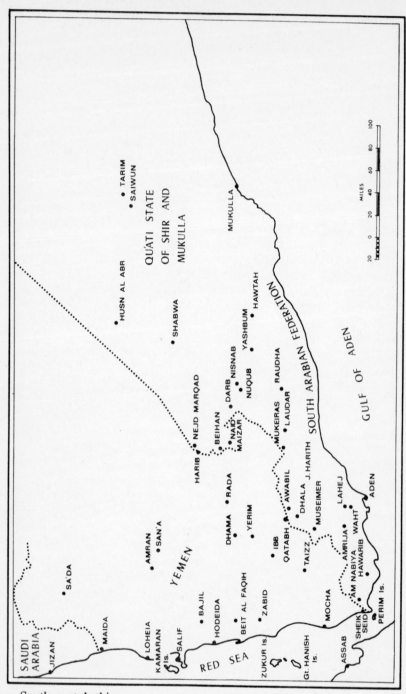

South-west Arabia

1

EARLY EUROPEAN INTEREST IN THE YEMEN

(i) PORTUGAL THE TRAIL BLAZER

The Portuguese established their first trading post in India at the beginning of the sixteenth century and soon founded a commercial settlement at Malacca in the East Indies. To consolidate their supremacy in the field, they preyed on Arab and Venetian shipping in the Red Sea and attempted a blockade in order to suppress these rivals who carried silks and spices from the East to Cairo and so to the Mediterranean for distribution in Europe. Although the Portuguese empire in the East flourished during the sixteenth century, it was never successful – because of the opposition of the Mameluke and later the Ottoman navies – in establishing itself in the Red Sea. In spite of attempts to subdue Aden and to rally the Abyssinian Christians to assist in attacking the Arabian coast, Ormuz in the Persian Gulf remained its nearest stronghold to the Arabian Peninsula for a hundred years.

Having managed in the fourteenth century to free herself from her Moorish conquerors, Portugal took up the mantle of the old Crusaders by trying to encircle the Islamic world. Prince Henry, who died in 1540, missed seeing this aim fulfilled, in Vasco da Gama's voyage to India, by some thirty-seven years. Before the end of 1520 there had already been considerable Portuguese activity off the Arabian coast and in the Red Sea, principally in connection with the landing of their missions to the Abyssinian king. As early as 1509 Gregorio da Quadra was captured at Zeila and was sent with some companions to Zabid in the Yemen where he was released some years later together with the only five who remained alive. Da Quadra made a long journey through Arabia, finally returning to Portugal in 1520. Albuquerque, having already occupied Socotra in 1507, attempted to take Aden in March 1513; he failed, encamped at Kamaran and later landed at Perim. His successor, Lope Soarez, decided to capture Aden on his return from a voyage up the Red Sea in 1517. He failed to take Jedda and, retiring to Kamaran, much of his force died. He found Aden strong enough to resist him effectively when his fleet emerged once more into the Indian Ocean. Thereafter the Portuguese voyages to the Red Sea were to be confined to reconnaissances of the naval activities of the Turks, who used Suez as a base and the Red Sea as a haven for their fleets set on attacking India. The fleet of Diego Lopes de Sequeira landed an envoy at Massawa (now in Eritrea) in 1520 but did not touch upon the Arabian coast. Sulaiman Pasha took Aden for the Turks in 1538. Four years later the last big Portuguese fleet entered the Red Sea, and on this occasion Dom Cristovao da Gama and twelve others were captured in Abyssinia. Da Gama was killed but some of his fellow prisoners were sent to Zabid. In 1547, Aden could have become a Portuguese possession when a local Arab chief, Ali Sulaiman al Tawlaki, ousted the Turks and asked the Portuguese for assistance. Payo de Noronha, who was sent to hold the town, retreated when Ali was overthrown by the Turks and, when Joao de Castro sent his son to help, the Turks under the famous Piri Rais had already retaken the town.

Most Portuguese who penetrated into the Yemen were captives or missionaries. Fernao Mendez Pinto was taken to Mocha in 1540 after being captured by the Turks with eleven others in the Red Sea; after spending some months in the town as a slave, he managed to make his way to Ormuz and thence to Goa. Roque de Brito was taken to Sana by the Turks who had captured him off East Africa in 1586. In the same year Ruy Goncalves de Camara anchored near Mocha and sent men ashore to explore the town but, unable to burn Mocha as he had intended, he landed a large party to obtain water. Pedro Paez and Antonio de Monserrat, two Spanish Jesuit Fathers, having been captured off the Kuria Muria Islands in February 1590 while on their way from Muscat to Zeila, were taken ashore near Salalah and sent to Sana via the Wadi Hadramaut. After spending five and a half years in Sana they were sent through Taizz to Mocha where they passed another year before being finally ransomed. By this time the power of the Portuguese was already on the wane. In Muscat and on the East African coast they had already received devastating attacks from Mocha at the hands of the fleet of the Turkish officer Ali Bey. Portugal's power and sovereignty had been all but eclipsed by her defeat in the Battle of Alcazar–Kebir in Morocco in 1578. The Netherlands seceded from King Philip II in the following year, and a weakened Spain

incorporated a defeated Portugal and her dominions under the
Spanish crown in 1580. Portuguese fortunes were thenceforward
inevitably bound up with those of Spain, with the consequence
that her hegemony in the East could not long survive the first
decade of the seventeenth century.

(ii) THE ENGLISH EAST INDIA COMPANY 1599–1663

The English East India Company, which was chartered in 1599,
soon broke the Portuguese monopoly in the Indian Ocean; eventually, with the support of Persian troops, it captured Ormuz
from its Portuguese defenders in 1621. The first voyage of the
chartered company through the Indian Ocean in 1601 was
preceded by that of James Lancaster, captain of the *Edward
Bonaventure*, who left Plymouth on April 10, 1591, rounded the
Cape and, passing Socotra, sailed to the East Indies. The
Company's second voyage, under Sir Henry Middleton, was made
three years after the first. By the end of 1606 only these two small
fleets had been despatched from England and only one factory,
at Bantam in Java, had been established. Progress had been
disappointingly slow, and the markets for English manufactured
goods had scarcely been extended. In the light of the success which
the newly formed Dutch East India Company had achieved in the
Indian Ocean, and because of the failure of two English attempts
to reach China by the north-west, matters took on a new urgency.
The first two voyages had brought home spices, it is true, but only
in return for bullion. Because it became clear that barter trading
was required, and some wider choice of return cargoes appeared
necessary, it was decided to open up relations with the dominions
of the Mughal Emperor and, as a second consideration, with the
Red Sea ports – themselves much frequented by Indian trading
vessels. William Keeling, in command of the ensuing third voyage
of the Company, reached Socotra in 1608 whence he tried to
reach Aden to establish a factory; but contrary winds thwarted
him and he took the *Dragon* on to Bantam whilst his second in
command, William Hawkins, departed in the *Hector* for the
Indian coast. On August 24, 1608, the *Hector* anchored off Surat,
the first English ship to visit an Indian port.

In the meantime, in 1607, the Company had raised a stock of
£33,000 for a fourth voyage. The *Ascension* (Captain Alexander

Sharpie) was purchased for this expedition, and she sailed from England in company with the *Union* the following year. The *Union* found her way to Sumatra and on April 7, 1609, the *Ascension* reached Aden only to find it a place of no trade and to receive obstruction at the hands of the Turkish governor. Consequently Sharpie sent two of his officers, William Revett and Phillip Glascock, to Mocha in a native boat in order to examine the trading prospects for indigo. Trade at Mocha was desultory and John Jourdain, whom Sharpie sent from Aden to the Turkish pasha at Sana to settle customs duties to be paid on goods landed at Aden, failed to obtain permission to establish a factory either at Mocha or at Aden. Sir Henry Middleton, coming out as 'general' of the East India Company's sixth voyage aboard the *Trades Increases*, and having left this ship at Aden, arrived at Mocha on November 13, 1610, with the *Peppercorn* (Nicholas Downton), the *Darling* (William Pemberton) and a 180-ton victualler, the *Samuel*. Attempts to trade were unsuccessful and Sir Henry Middleton, Pemberton, Femel, Benjamin Green (a factor of the *Darling*) and thirty-one others were taken in captivity via Taizz to Sana, a journey which took them fifteen days. On January 17, 1611, John Fowler and eighteen others arrived at Sana from the *Trades Increases* which was moored off Aden, and, having spent a month in the city, the two parties set out for Mocha via Dhamar, Yerim and Taizz. Sir Henry reached the ships off Mocha after a somewhat hazardous escape in a barrel and brought his guns to threaten the port. The remainder of the company were able to get aboard and on June 24 the vessels left the Mocha roads and stood for Kamaran.

The next year sailing from India in the spring with the *Trades Increases*, *Darling* and *Peppercorn*, Sir Henry Middleton plundered Indian shipping at the mouth of the Red Sea. At the time of the capture of these Indian ships the *Clove* (John Saris), *Hector* (Gabriel Towerson) and *Thomas* of the Company's eighth voyage under John Saris were anchored in the Mocha roads. Although he was received more favourably than Sir Henry had been, Saris found that he was unable to obtain permission to trade, although he possessed a letter from the Turks at Constantinople guaranteeing him safe conduct in Arabia. This was mainly due to Sir Henry's behaviour on his previous visit. One of Saris' merchants, Richard Wickham, brought letters to Sir Henry, then in the Straits of

Bab-el-Mandeb, explaining the situation. Later, Saris with his three ships joined Sir Henry at sea, and complained that the latter's plundering exploits had resulted in the merchants of Mocha refusing to trade with him. Saris and Sir Henry eventually agreed upon the sharing of the booty from the Indian ships, but not without 'very grosse speeches not fittinge for men of their rank'. John Jourdain had accompanied Sir Henry Middleton on this voyage and in May, when the disputes between the 'generals' of the two voyages were still raging, he sailed for Sumatra in the *Darling* with John Fowler, one of Sir Henry's merchants, in search of pepper, and carrying a cargo of cloth. In April 1618, Andrew Shilling, with Joseph Salbanke, William Baffin, Edward Haynes and Richard Barker, returned from Surat as master of the *Royal Anne* under the direction of Sir Thomas Roe, having established better relations. Shilling had obtained a firman from the Imam of Sana and the Governor of Mocha permitting the English to trade in any Yemeni port while Salbanke, one of the merchants of this voyage, was sent to Sana on June 23, 1618, and returned on July 27, with the necessary authority and the news that in Taizz there was a body of between thirty and forty thousand soldiers commanded by a German renegade. The establishment of the first English factory and residency at Mocha can be dated from this time; this residency was only finally abolished in 1828. The *Royal Anne* left for Surat on August 20, 1618, Sir Thomas Roe returning home in the same vessel, leaving Surat on February 17, 1619. On the same day the *Lion* sailed for Mocha with letters to the governor from Sir Thomas, and her cargo was sold at Mocha at a hundred per cent profit before the ship returned to Surat in October 1619. Three more ships with Salbanke and Haynes as chief merchants were sent from Surat to Mocha in March 1622 and were favourably received, in the following year a further three were also welcomed at Mocha. However, by 1640 the depredation of pirates had brought the Mocha–India trade to a standstill.

Coffee, grown in the hinterland of the Red Sea coast of the Yemen, had been mentioned by Jourdain and Revett as likely to be a beneficial item of trade as early as 1609. The Dutch, through Pieter van den Broecke, were to be made aware of it in 1616, but it was not until 1628 that they bought their first forty bales. In 1661 the first consignment arrived in Amsterdam. The English East India Company did not begin to show an interest in coffee until 1627, when the Court of Directors was informed by William Burt, their agent in Isfahan, that 'the seedes and the huske, both of which are useful in making the drinke, were found only at Moka, although the beverage is used in Turkey and in other parts of Arabia, Persia and India'. On February 27, 1630, Burt wrote to the Company: 'If the ships go to Moka with a well chosen cargo they will do well, especially if the proceeds be invested in Cowa (coffee) seeds which find vente in Suratt and Persia unto your large advantage.' Coffee did not reach England until 1650, nor appear in the Company's sales lists until 1660. However, the English factory at Mocha proved unprofitable and in 1660 the Company ordered it to be 'wholly deserted' and coffee to be obtained from Basra. Herbert Hugo, a Dutch pirate captain of the *Black Eagle*, who, in the spring of 1662, burned several dhows and larger vessels in the Mocha roads, under the eyes of the governor, and then proceeded to loot the town, hastened the English withdrawal. English factors were among his victims and several thousands of pounds were taken from them. The raids of Hugo had such a disastrous effect that in 1663 the English factory was 'dismantled, locked and barred' by Anthony Smith, the Company's agent at Mocha.

England had desired to trade in the Red Sea because bilateral commerce had many serious drawbacks, not the least of which was the need to export specie on a grand scale from England. For the English, Red Sea commerce developed into a carrying trade from India to foreign merchants at Mocha who paid largely in cash. Mocha, for the coffee trade, became a branch of the Company's factory at Bandar Abbas at the head of the Persian Gulf. However, the reorganisation of the Company just after the middle of the seventeenth century was followed by the closing of the Mocha factory because experience had shown that native shipping executed the Company's coastal carrying trade more cheaply and more efficiently. The English factory was soon reopened, however, and remained established with several interruptions until the early years of the nineteenth century.

(iii) THE DUTCH EAST INDIA COMPANY 1602–1800

At the end of the sixteenth century the dense population of the Netherlands was about half that of England. Having liberated herself from the Spanish crown in 1581, the Dutch could embark upon overseas commercial enterprises in competition with the English and Portuguese. The first Dutch fleet to round the Cape sailed in 1595 and the Dutch East India Company was formed in 1602. It was not, however, until later that a ship was sent to Arabia, in August 1614 when Pieter van den Broecke in the *Nassau* tried unsuccessfully to open a factory at Aden. Eighteen months later, sailing from Bantam and having called at Shihr on the south Arabian coast to visit the two merchants he had previously left there, he put into the Mocha roads in the *Nassau* in January 1616. The establishment of the Dutch factory at Mocha was the result of Pieter van den Broecke's pioneering work. He and Jan Arentsz journeyed through Taizz, Yarim and Dhamar to Sana and, having made a trade agreement favourable to the Dutch East India Company, sailed from Mocha on July 7. Van den Broecke returned to Aden in the *'t Wapen van Zeelandt* on August 22, 1620, and later sailed for Socotra, having left an upper-merchant Herman van Gil and two assistants in Aden to trade. After staying there a month van Gil left Aden for Sana on September 26, and arrived on October 15. He remained for a fortnight in the capital and arrived back at Aden on November 10 and at Mocha on January 21, 1621.

Although Van den Broecke traded at Mocha in 1616, the Dutch were unable to obtain permission from the Ottoman Government to establish a factory there until July 1618. Further Dutch ships sailing into the Red Sea in 1620 plundered craft from Portuguese India in the Straits of Bab-el-Mandeb, an action of which the Turks took a serious view: as a reprisal, the stocks of the Dutch factory were confiscated and the staff imprisoned. The factor, Willem de Milde, was never completely released from his captivity and the Dutch factory never recovered from the effect of this dispute. On July 4, the *Weesp* and *Sampson* (Captain Pieter Gillisz van Ravesteyn) arrived at Mocha when those on shore learned that Captain van Ravesteyn had died at sea, it was arranged that de Milde should take his place. Van Gil, who had received the *Weesp* at Mocha, died on July 14, and de Milde then became the chief Dutch factor at the port. He and three other Dutchmen set out for Zabid on February 16, 1622, but when they arrived thirteen days later they were imprisoned and Willem Cornelisz Cuycken and five others at Mocha were arrested. De Milde was, however, released shortly afterward and he returned to Mocha on March 20. On his arrival he found the *'t Wapen van Zeelandt* and the *Noord Holland* under the command of Jan van Gorcum. Albert Becker and twenty sailors from the *'t Wapen van Zeelandt* who went ashore were arrested, and de Milde and the other factors were taken as captives to Sana by the Pasha, Ahmad Fazli. De Milde arrived back at Mocha on August 6, and Becker and the sailors sailed with van Gorcum in the *'t Wapen van Zeelandt* and *Noord Holland* on August 19.

François Lemmens in the *Heusden* arrived at Mocha on March 12, 1623, to take away the cash in hand at the Dutch factory but sailed with no more than 4,000 riyals on April 28. De Milde was then forced to visit Sana again and in August he spent a fortnight at Zabid.

Herman van Speult with the *Mauritius, Oranje, Walcheren, Gouden Leeuw, Hollandia, Engelsche Beer* and *Goede Fortuin* arrived at Mocha in June 1626 from the Moluccas and sent two Dutch merchants to Sana in mid-July. They returned to Mocha after unsuccessful trade negotiations to find that van Speult had died on July 23 and that the ships had set sail for India on August 10, leaving de Milde still a prisoner at Taizz. Two years later on May 15, 1628, Job Christiaensz Grijp arrived at Mocha in command of the *Bommel* and the *Weesp*. He was unsuccessful in arranging the release of de Milde and as there was little trade he sailed with forty bags of coffee and some other merchandise on July 12.

Attempts that were made the following year to re-establish the factory were abandoned, and only an intermittent trade continued. Between 1648 and 1652 the Dutch brought coffee from Mocha for their establishments in North-west India and Persia but it was not until 1661 that it was first sold in Amsterdam, being shipped direct to Holland from Mocha for the first time two years later. Varying amounts reached Amsterdam direct each year until 1667, when shipments ceased. In 1684 it was decided to discontinue trading to Mocha, and orders for coffee during that decade were directed to the Company's factories in Persia and at Surat.

Occasional visits were, however, made until in 1696 a Dutch factory was re-established at the port under Nicholaas Welters and Adriaen van den Heuvel. After some lean years in 1702–6 and 1710–12, trade reached a peak in 1720. Abraham Pantzer and Gabriel Scholten had already been installed at the factory as

residents but in February 1719 they were replaced by Jan van
Leeuwen, Pieter Zeegers and Jan van Alderweereld, who arrived
aboard the *Vrieswijck* and the *Amsterdam*. The *Vrieswijck* was fully
loaded with coffee by June 27. The following year the *Rotterdam*
and the *Lugtenberg* took back the largest consignment of coffee
ever to be shipped from Mocha by the Dutch. In 1721 90 per cent
of Dutch coffee had come from Mocha; five years later the same
proportion came from Java. In the meantime, in 1724, the
residency was disestablished; however, visits to the port were still
necessary as an outlet for Dutch goods, and trading was done from
the ships themselves. Only one ship was sent in 1725 and by 1730
there was such a glut of coffee in Europe that only very small
amounts were bought by the Dutch at Mocha. The Company
again decided to close the factory in 1738 as coffee was obtainable
much more cheaply from Java; yet the factory building was
retained by the Dutch throughout the eighteenth century,
although sometimes no Dutch ship visited Mocha for two or
three years at a time. By the beginning of the nineteenth century
it had long been abandoned.

By the end of the seventeenth century the Dutch had lost their
position as a major power, and the English, who hitherto had
possessed no more than a foothold in the East, were able to take
their place. Sharp competition between England and Holland had
only begun after 1660. A great deal of the Dutch success had been
due to England's absorption, throughout much of the century,
in constitutional and religious problems; but the strain of wars
with England and later with France had sapped Dutch vitality
too far. Meanwhile Colbert, the enterprising minister of Louis XIV,
laid plans for the creation of France's future commercial empire
across the seas.

(iv) THE FRENCH IN THE RED SEA 1665-1789

Since the fourteenth century, French sailors had been running
down the coast of West Africa. As far back as 1272 Lancelot
Maloizel reconnoitred the Canaries and in 1402 a Norman gentle-
man, Jean de Béthencourt, leading a small group of adventurers,
took possession of them. This act was officially approved by Henry
III of Castile. An early French attempt to reach India by sea was
made in 1503 by Captain Paulmier de Gonneville of Honfleur,

who sailed in command of the *Espoir* in an endeavour to round the Cape; blown off course by storms, he ended up on the coast of Brazil. In 1529 two ships were fitted out at Dieppe by Jean Ango; the project was initiated by the brothers Jean and Raoul Parmentier who captained the two ships *Pensée* of 200 tons and the *Sacré* of 120 tons. The Parmentier brothers aimed to reach China but some members of their crews were massacred on the coast of Madagascar, and when they reached Sumatra the two captains and most of their sailors died of fever.

Although these early ventures were unsuccessful, the disaster of the Parmentier brothers had the effect of replacing royal indifference to such projects by official encouragement. This took the form of declarations by François I in 1537 and 1542 aimed at publishing the royal approval of any desirable maritime enterprise. However, French effort in this direction was temporarily retarded by the religious wars in which France was involved at the end of the sixteenth century. Henri III continued the policy of François I with a royal declaration published in 1578, but no advantage was taken of this mark of royal interest. Under Henri IV France was once more at peace, and overseas trading again came into its own. At the turn of the sixteenth century large numbers of ships were based on the French channel ports. One merchant, Pierre Vampérine of Rouen, owned seventeen ships with which he traded to the East and West Indies. A company was formed at St. Malo in 1601 by some merchants of St. Malo, Laval and Vitré for trading exclusively with the East Indies. They fitted out the *Croissant* (Captain La Bardelière) and the *Corbin* (Captain Groût du Clos-Neuf). The voyage went well until the *Corbin* was wrecked on the Maldive Islands, where the Dutch and Portuguese were so hostile to the crew of the *Croissant* that she returned without a cargo.

In spite of all their failures these early pioneers laid the foundations of the greater efforts which were to be made in the future. The government of Henri IV, feeling compelled to imbue French commerce and industry with new life, followed with interest the creation of the English and Dutch chartered trading companies. As a result, much encouragement was given to the formation of a company headed by an experienced Flemish captain, Gerard Le Roy, and assisted by a Limoges financier, Antoine Godefroy. Brest was designated as this company's port to enable its vessels to fly the royal standard, thus giving them the status of a royal fleet. Ships were built and crewed by Dutchmen and four of the vessels were fitted out at St. Malo. These preparations came to nought but at least the company's royal privilege, obtained in 1611, was confirmed for a tenure of twelve years by letters patent. Several more companies were formed with scant success during the following years, until the government combined their efforts into the *Compagnie des Moluques*. It fell to Richelieu, who became Superintendent of Commerce and the Navy in 1627, to found the original French East India Company. On June 24, 1642, he obtained a royal charter for ten years for a company to establish colonies in Madagascar and other adjacent islands and to take possession of them in the name of the King. The letters patent officially designated the company as the *Compagnie d'Orient* but it lasted barely twenty years, and Colbert reconstituted it on the lines of the English and Dutch companies in 1664, with the style of *Compagnie des Indes Orientales*. During the next four years several Frenchmen settled at Surat and by 1670 François Martin had laid the foundations of the French colony at Pondicherry. Once again the chartered company foundered, re-emerging as the *Compagnie Perpetuel des Indes*. The son of a director of this company, Joseph Dupleix, was to guide the destinies of the French in India: he developed French commerce in Bengal and established trading relations with China, Jedda and Mocha.

The oriental aspirations of France, like those of England, had existed for a long time but the French, comparatively, were late comers to the Red Sea. Antoine Beaulieu, who reached Java after sailing from Honfleur in 1616, had sailed along the south Arabian coast in 1620. Then, in 1665 the *St. Paul*, sailing from Brest, tried to reach Mocha and Socotra from Madagascar in order to obtain news of the envoys of Louis XIV to the King of Persia and the Great Mughal but was prevented from entering the Red Sea by the north-west monsoon. It remained for a Malouin vessel to take the honours of being the first French ship to call at Mocha. On January 6, 1708, the *Curieux* (de Merveille) and *Diligent* (Champloret) weighed anchor at Brest, and arrived before Mocha a year later on January 3, 1709. The Frenchmen were entertained by the director of the Dutch factory at Mocha and a commercial treaty was made between the French and the Mocha governor, and a factory established. The company of merchants of

St. Malo, which had financed the expedition, dispatched the *Diligent* (Briselaine) and the *Paix* (de la Lande) in January 1710. They arrived at Mocha on December 2, having captured three ships, two English and one Dutch, en route. Barbier, surgeon of the *Diligent*, and Major de la Grelaudière made a long journey inland to the Imam at Muab to attend to his ailments. Some trading was done at Mocha.

In 1710 the merchants of St. Malo decided to send their ships to Mocha and to India alternately, and in 1714 the commercial activity of the Malouins proceeded apace. Early in that year the *Chasseur* and the *Paix* sailed for Mocha and in November the *Auguste* was also sent there. The *Chasseur* was late in arriving, having take possession of Mauritius en route in September 1715, but she and the *Paix* returned to St. Malo from Mocha in February 1716. In the following year the *Comtesse de Pontchartrain*, the last vessel sent from St. Malo direct to Mocha for a long time, started off on a two-year voyage to the Indies finally returning in May 1719. But relations between the French and the Mocha authorities were to become strained. Realising that, while most European nations paid a 5 per cent customs duty on imports and exports, the French under their treaty of 1709 were paying only $\frac{1}{4}$ per cent, Faqi Ahmad, the Governor of Mocha, raised the French customs duty to 5 per cent without notice. Much incensed by this high-handed action the French East India Company decided to take punitive action. It selected Captain de la Garde-Jazier – nephew of Admiral Duguay-Trouin, hero of the French capture of Rio de Janeiro in 1711 – to command the squadron which was to be despatched from St. Malo. Four ships comprised the little fleet: the *Maurépas* (de la Garde-Jazier), the *Heron* (Captain Bachelier), the *St. Pierre* and the *Indien*. Mocha was bombarded in 1737 by the squadron and as a result Mocha paid its debts to the French and promised to abide by the 1709 treaty.

French interest in the Mocha coffee trade soon declined, however. As far back as 1711, the *Paix* and the *Diligent* had taken Yemeni coffee bushes for propagation in Réunion. By mid-century France had become involved in a fierce struggle with the English in India, and after 1761 her hopes of an Indian empire were shattered. Anglo–French rivalry continued in Egypt in a struggle for control of the Red Sea communications, and French movements in the Red Sea for some decades were made solely in support of this rivalry. In 1785 the French frigate *Auguste* called at Suez with despatches; in the following year five French ships were at Mocha, and in 1787 the *Vénus* delivered further despatches at Suez, having carried out an extensive survey of the Red Sea. French interest in the Yemen remained desultory, however, in spite of the visits to Mocha of *La Louise Julie* of the Société de la Mer Rouge in 1788, and the *Prince de Condé* and the *Amis Réunis* in 1789.

There were smaller nations with which, during the eighteenth century, France, Holland and England had to contend in the eastern seas. Not the least of these were, for a short time, the Belgians. The Royal and Imperial East India Company established in the Austrian Netherlands, to give the Ostend Company its full title, was founded in 1717, and letters patent were granted by the Emperor Charles VI in 1722. The Company's ships carried out a considerable trade at Mocha between 1719 and 1727, much to the embarrassment of the French, Dutch and English. The governments of those countries, however, soon contrived to overcome their common adversary, forcing Charles VI to suppress its activities. The Ostenders had in a short time founded a substantial trading organisation near Madras and at Bankibazar on the Ganges, but the Danes had preceded them there by a hundred years. A chartered Danish company was constituted by Christian IV in 1612, and Serampore and Tranquebar were founded by it on the Coromandel coast eight years later. This company was ruined by Dutch hostility but further companies were formed in 1634, 1686 and 1728. Intermittent trading was done at Mocha by the Danes in the seventeenth century, but it never reached any significant proportions. King Gustavus Adolphus was the driving force behind the formation of the Swedish East India Company, and some Swedish forts were built and occupied for a time on the west coast of Africa. The Swedish company had a factory at Canton, but occasionally traded at Mocha during the latter part of the eighteenth century.

(v) THE ROUTE TO INDIA

During the three hundred years from 1500 to 1800 only four European nations contributed substantially to the course of events in the Indian Ocean. For a century the Portuguese were unencumbered by other European nations and, while they failed in their chief design of outflanking the Muslim world, trade was for them only a secondary consideration. Arriving in the eastern seas at the beginning of the seventeenth century after the Portuguese decline, the Dutch and the English continued for more than a hundred years to trade unhampered except by each other. For both nations trade with the Yemen, while important, was of far less consequence than that with India or the East Indies. Neither Aden nor Mocha was of interest as a way station for revictualling, because ships would pass directly from East Africa or Zanzibar to India. Early in the eighteenth century French traders appeared in the Yemen to compete with the already established Dutch and English commerce. From 1720 until about 1730 European trade at Mocha, intensified by the interloping activities of the smaller nations, reached record proportions and then, over the next sixty years, steadily declined. In the meantime events remote from South-western Arabia were beginning to affect the policies of England and France. By 1750 Dutch competition had long ceased to be effective and such Anglo-French rivalry as there had been in the Red Sea moved from the area of commerce to that of communications. Since the discovery of the Cape route, England had progressively neglected the Levant trade, and had latterly pursued a policy of maintaining friendly relations with, and upholding the sovereignty of, the ailing Ottoman Empire. The aim had been to avoid its downfall and the consequent rush of European rivals to fill the vacuum. The French, however, were prepared to antagonise the Ottoman Government if such was necessary to protect their trading interests. They had become well established in Egypt by the beginning of the eighteenth century, at which time the volume of their Egyptian trade was twenty-five times greater than that of England, and they maintained a virtual European monopoly of Egyptian trade throughout most of the eighteenth century. When France lost her Indian empire after the Seven Years War, she immediately sought to consolidate her position in Egypt, where she contrived to establish a base from which to regain her lost possessions in India. In 1785 she signed a secret treaty with the Mameluke beys of Egypt which gave her, among other rights, shipping privileges in the Red Sea. During this period a large number of both French and English ships carried out the first primitive maritime surveys. Anglo-French rivalry in Egypt quickly developed into a contest for the acquisition of exclusive concessions for the overland carriage of despatches between Suez and the Mediterranean; but the advent of the French Revolution, and the European wars which followed, diverted the attention of both French and English from the overland route and from the Suez Canal projects which were later to have such far-reaching effects upon world commerce, and which were already in embryo.

Napoleon's occupation of Egypt began in the autumn of 1798. Suddenly, after two centuries of exclusively commercial intercourse with the Yemen, the British Government was forced to take swift political action in South-west Arabia – the first such move in European history.

2

THE CHANGE FROM TRADE
TO POLITICS

(i) NAVAL OPERATIONS 1799–1801

French presence in Egypt dictated two changes in the British position in the Red Sea: first, the dispatch of an expeditionary force to land on the Red Sea coast of Egypt (to reinforce General Abercromby's Mediterranean Force) and secondly the seizure of a strategic point in the Red Sea from which all enemy shipping in those narrow waters could be controlled. Destined to play the major part in these military and political moves were three officers: Admiral John Blankett, who was sent from England to patrol the Red Sea in command of a squadron consisting of the *Leopard* (Captain T. Surridge), the *Daedalus* and the *Orestes*; Commodore Sir Home Popham, in command of a squadron comprising the *Romney*, the *Victor* and the *Sensible*, who was to escort convoys of troops from both the Cape and Bombay to the Red Sea coast of Egypt; and Lieutenant Colonel (later General Sir) John Murray, who was to occupy the island of Perim with a contingent of troops and to receive the title of Political Commissioner for the Red Sea.

Having visited Madagascar in 1789 Admiral Blankett was no newcomer to the Indian Ocean. He left Portsmouth on July 9, 1798, but, being delayed by storms in the Atlantic and therefore unable to round the Cape until early October, he eventually became stranded on the East African coast by contrary winds. The *Daedalus* was sent back to the Cape for provisions, with orders to rejoin the squadron at Aden, the *Leopard* and *Orestes* finally putting into Mocha on April 14, 1799, only to find that the *Centurion* (Captain J. S. Rainier) and *Albatross* (Captain W. Waller) had already been sent to Suez by the Commander-in-Chief, East Indies. In the meantime the *Fox*, *Princess Charlotte*, *Strombolo* and some transports and gunboats took Lieutenant-Colonel Murray with 200 Europeans of the 84th Regiment and 600 native troops to occupy Perim. Murray landed on the island on May 3, 1799, setting up a permanent garrison there, but when Blankett arrived on May 7 he found the garrison ill equipped, short of water and unable, with the guns supplied, to command the Straits of Bab-el-Mandeb. Accordingly, Murray moved his garrison to Aden and, arriving on September 1, was welcomed by the Abdali Sultan, Ahmad bin Abdul-Karim, who offered his territory to the British.

Blankett arrived at Bombay from the Red Sea in January 1800, and tried to persuade the Bombay government to accept Aden as a gift and to maintain a garrison there. He pointed out that as the majority of Arabian revenues, which came from coffee and the pilgrim traffic, were spent on the purchase of cereals from Egypt, British possession of Aden could control the food supplies of the western half of Arabia, and also divert the Mocha coffee trade through Aden itself. However, this great opportunity was turned down by the Governor-General of India in February 1800, and Murray's force, after spending five months in Aden, sailed for Bombay in March. Blankett also returned to the Red Sea in March with the *Leopard*, *Forte*, *Fox*, *Albatross* and *Amboyna* with orders to thwart any French designs for using Egypt as a base for invading India. Finding Aden and Perim devoid of their garrisons he held a meeting in June with the Sherif of Mecca and managed to persuade him to withhold any assistance from the French. He continued to blockade Suez and in August returned once more to Bombay. In April 1801 he was again at Suez and in June assisted Commodore Sir Home Popham in disembarking at Kosseir (on the west coast of the Red Sea) the troops which Popham had convoyed from India and the Cape.

(ii) SIR HOME POPHAM'S EMBASSY, 1802

Sir Home Riggs Popham, the first Englishman authorised to carry out official political negotiations with the Imam of the Yemen, was born in 1762. His career in the Royal Navy was eventful and unorthodox. In his earlier years he had shown himself to be a man of initiative and enterprise and, possessing that quality essential to efficiency – an eye for relevant detail – had won favour with senior officials of the government at home. In 1794 he spent some time under the Duke of York in Flanders conveying dispatches to and from England, and for the duration of that appointment he was much consulted by His Majesty's ministers, enjoying considerable influence with them. As a captain he was appointed in 1800 to command the *Romney* of fifty guns, leader of the small squadron ordered to convoy the troops to Egypt from the Cape of Good Hope and from India. These were the forces which were to act in conjunction with General Abercromby's Mediterranean force to expel the French from Egypt. On May 7, 1801, Popham was off Mocha aboard the *Romney* attended by the *Victor* and *Sensible* (Captain Sause). On the following day he took the *Romney* and sailed in company with the *Victor* to Jedda to meet General Baird, the commander of the Red Sea expeditionary force to Egypt. Sir Home arrived at Jedda on May 26 and took the General to Kosseir, the southern port of disembarkation for the invasion of Egypt, arriving there on June 7 to find that Colonel Murray, lately commander of the Perim garrison, was already there. Blankett was then at Suez and arrived at Kosseir on June 16 with a letter from General Sir Hely Hutchinson, whose army was before Cairo, asking for the rapid dispatch of the Indian contingent. Admiral Blankett immediately left for Jedda and when Popham arrived there on July 6 he found the Admiral so ill that he was completely unable to deal with official matters; he died aboard the *Leopard* on July 14 on the way to Mocha.

Dr. Pringle, an assistant surgeon in the Bombay Government, who had accompanied Murray to the Red Sea in 1799, was at Mocha in May 1801, and Popham sent him to Sana with letters and 30,000 rupees' worth of shawls, satins and muslins as presents for the Imam. Pringle arranged help for British ships in Yemeni ports, the restoration of trading concessions previously enjoyed, and permission for a naval hospital to be established at Mocha. For all his good work, however, Pringle later fell from grace, for in March 1805 'an unfortunate attachment to spirituous liquors had so greatly gained on him, that everything at the factory was thrown into confusion'. He seems to have returned to Bombay later in 1805 after six continuous years' service at Mocha – a test of character for any European.

At the beginning of August 1801 Sir Home arrived back in India and, reporting to the Governor-General, received from him, towards the end of the year, his appointment as ambassador to the States of Arabia. He had received previous instructions from the Secret Committee of the East India Company to enter into some system of lasting commercial relations with the Imam of Sana and the Sherif of Mecca. Before Popham's departure from England, the Secretary of the Committee, Henry Dundas, had given him a political appointment to the Sherif of Mecca and 'all the Arabian Princes'. He had been able to observe during his earlier visit to Mocha something of the commercial situation in the Yemen and, in a long paper on the subject to the Governor-General, had recommended that a British commercial resident be established at the port. At Beit al-Faqih a commercial fair was held twice yearly; this fair, said Sir Home, should be attended by the commercial resident. For many years prior to 1800 an Indian Banian had transacted the East India Company's business in the Yemen.

At the end of 1801 Sir Home Popham finally received his detailed terms of reference from the Governor-General, Lord Wellesley, and, being duly appointed once more as ambassador to the States of Arabia, set sail early in 1802. He arrived at Suez in March intending to travel to Cairo to conclude a commercial treaty with the Pasha of Egypt; he had also intended to visit General Baird at Alexandria to discuss troop embarkation arrangements, but he was prevented from doing either by the prevalence of plague in Cairo. He returned to Jedda late in June and, by the middle of July, had once again dropped anchor in the Mocha roads. From there he again sent Dr. Pringle, this time accompanied by W. P. Elliot and Lieutenant Lamb, to Sana to negotiate a commercial treaty with the Imam. The Governor-General knowing perhaps about his arrogant nature, had thought it wiser for Sir Home to remain at Mocha and had instructed him not to proceed inland unless some special advantage would thereby be gained. While Sir Home was waiting at Mocha, he recorded that there would be no difficulty in the provision of a factory at the town as the Dutch factory had been given up many years previously because of the continual disputes in which the Dutch had been involved with the Mocha government; it seems that the Dutch factory had remained empty for many years and could with some additions have answered the British purpose. The old English factory was in ruins, and Sir Home thought it desirable to procure another house of equal size or to obtain the Imam's permission to build a new one. If this were not allowed, he wished to have a number of 'nuisances' near the English factory removed and, if the land where the ruins stood, the governor's stables and the public gaol could all be purchased and added to the old English factory, a satisfactory building could be constructed.

From India there was considerable opposition to Sir Home Popham's embassy. The Nawab of Surat, through his agent at Sana, tried hard to prevent the regeneration of the factory at Mocha and indeed the revival of British trade in the Red Sea, which was an important aim of Sir Home's mission; the Nawab had also tried to prevent the landing of any of the embassy's escort. Popham eventually managed to find an excuse to penetrate inland, but having set out from Mocha he only reached Taizz. He was insultingly treated throughout his journey (mainly because he insisted on taking his own guard of 100 sepoys) and was forced to return to Mocha. As to Pringle's mission, Elliot died of fever in Sana, and Lamb and Pringle returned to Mocha on September 15, 1802, with nothing to report beyond a polite reception. The mission had been a failure; the Imam did not like the pistols and sabres which Pringle took as presents, but he did issue orders that no French ship should receive supplies in any of his ports. Undaunted, Sir Home proceeded to Aden where he made a treaty with the Abdali Sultan, Ahmed bin Abdul-Karim, who had entertained Murray and his troops so well in the early months of 1800 and who had offered forthwith to conclude a treaty of alliance. Under the treaty which Popham signed with the Sultan, the port was declared open to British goods if they were carried in British ships. The treaty, a lengthy document, also provided for the special protection of British subjects, the establishment of a British factory and many other details – even to the provision of a Christian burial ground. In addition, the British promised protection to the Sultan's subjects if they were attacked by the French.

Returning to England in the *Romney* in 1803, Popham faced a most improperly conducted naval inquiry into the cost of refitting his ship at Calcutta. He was finally vindicated and, for a time, projects such as Fulton's submarine and Congreve's rocket battery were committed to his charge. But he was soon in trouble again for undertaking an unauthorised expedition to Buenos Aires from the Cape of Good Hope. He was reprimanded by court-martial in the following March, but the next year he took part in the expedition against Copenhagen, receiving the KCB in 1815. He died in 1820.

(iii) THE WAHABI THREAT 1806–11

The exhortations of Blankett and Popham had fallen on deaf ears at home and Popham's treaty was soon forgotten. The departure of Napoleon from Egypt and the death in 1799 of his great ally, Tipoo, Sultan of Mysore, had already weakened the British home government's political interest in the Red Sea, but the English factory at Mocha was still maintained well into the nineteenth century despite frequent difficulties with the Mocha authorities and the depredations of the puritanical and fanatic Wahabis of central Arabia. Between 1806 and 1811 the Wahabis, who had occupied Hodeida in 1804 with a force under Abd al-Hakal, overran the Tihama. (Egyptian forces under the command of Ibrahim Pasha, did not expel them until 1826, when they garrisoned Hodeida, Mocha and Zabid, and restored the nominal authority of the Imam of Sana.) Matters came to a head in December 1820 when a squadron under command of Captain J. R. Lumley in HMS *Topaz* bombarded Mocha and landed a small body of men to take possession of it. A treaty was made with the governor of Mocha establishing a residency but the agreement was never ratified by the Imam at Sana.

By 1832 British interest in the establishment of the overland route from Cairo to Suez and the sea route from Suez to India had long since revived. In that year the armies of Muhamad Ali, Viceroy of Egypt, who had fought the Wahabis in 1813–18, had consolidated their position at Mocha and the Viceroy had decided to extend his dominion over the whole of Arabia. Five years later he despatched considerable reinforcements to the peninsula: one army was sent to the Euphrates, one to central Arabia and a third to the Hejaz and the Yemen. All this time Egyptian activity in South Arabia had been kept under the watchful eye of the Bombay Marine, which was unable to prevent the Egyptians cornering half of the Mocha coffee trade for themselves and selling at high prices to the Americans who only made a first tentative appearance at Mocha in 1797, after having long been hampered in their seaborne commerce by imperial restrictions.

(iv) AMERICANS IN THE RED SEA 1798–1840

The launching of Winthrop's *Blessing of the Bay* at Medford in New England in 1631 marked the beginning of serious shipbuilding enterprise on the Atlantic seaboard of America. By restricting the Dutch carrying trade, and confining colonial commerce to English and colonial vessels, the Navigation Act of 1651 gave added impetus to shipbuilding activities all along the New England coast. Ten years later shipbuilding had become the leading industry of Newburyport, Ipswich, Gloucester, Beverley, Marblehead, Boston and Salem. Long before the turn of the seventeenth century American square-riggers had been seen in most ports of Europe and the West Indies, and were not unknown as far afield as Alexandretta and the Guinea coast. In 1691 imperial control of commerce was tightened, but after the Peace of Utrecht of 1713 another wave of prosperity was welcomed by American merchants. In Massachusetts about 125 vessels were launched annually; then, after the War of Independence, the figure dropped to about forty-five. In 1784 twelve out of the forty-five were built for the French *Compagnie des Indes* which was to be re-established by Charles Alexandre de Calonne in 1785; between 1785 and 1787, only fifteen or twenty ships were built annually.

Before 1775, Salem had been principally a fishing port. Privateering had given to her seafarers broader horizons and a greater ambition for trade and, ten years before the close of the century, she was the sixth city of America, and it was Salem which opened legitimate American trade with the East in 1788. In 1784 the 300-ton *Grand Turk* (Captain Jonathan Ingersoll) of twenty-two guns, reached the Cape of Good Hope. The Philadelphia ship *United States* was off Pondicherry late in December 1784, and four years later the *Atlantic* (Captain Henry Elkins) was the first Salem ship to reach Bombay and Calcutta, already visited by the *Chesapeake* (Captain John O'Donnell) in 1787. The *Atlantic* put into Whampoa Reach below Canton in October of the following year and the *Grand Turk*, on its next voyage, by then under Captain Ebenezer West, reached Mauritius in 1787. The voyages of these Salem ships and that of the *Astrea* (Captain James Magee) to Canton in 1789 produced a great demand for new ships, particularly in Salem, where new shipbuilding yards were established. Prosperity was returning to New England, although Boston and Salem between them so monopolised the eastern trade that little was left for Providence, New York, Philadelphia or Baltimore. Nevertheless Newburyport managed to acquire considerable wealth without the aid of oriental trade.

On the other side of the coin, a large surplus of tea in the go-downs of Boston and Salem in 1790 forced their merchants to seek new outlets of trade, with the result, to mention only one, that oriental goods were being re-exported to the Mediterranean. British depredations on American commerce between 1793 and 1794 cost New Englanders dear and any type of commerce became better than none. Typical of such reluctant measures was the hiring out to the *Vereenigde Ost-Indische Compagnie* (the Dutch East India Company) of the *Eliza*, from New York, the *Massachusetts*, from Boston, and the *Margaret*, from Salem, between 1798 and 1801 to take part in the Batavia-Nagasaki carrying trade. New markets were, however, being sought and the Red Sea coffee trade was one of these.

Probably the most skilful of all Salem shipbuilders at the beginning of the nineteenth century was Retire Beckett. In 1794 he built the ship *Recovery*, 284 tons, for Elias Haskett Derby, who, at that time, shared with the Crowninshield family the position of the greatest of all the Salem owners; and in 1796 Captain Joseph Ropes took the *Recovery* to Calcutta, and, via Mauritius, to Mocha in 1798. It was the first American vessel to call at one of the Arabian ports at the entrance to the Red Sea thus beating the *Enterprise* captained by Richard Cleveland – who had taken her out of Salem in 1797 bound for Mocha. He had only reached Le Havre when he received orders from the owners to return. Ropes was well received at Mocha but having had little trading success, he went on to Calcutta, eventually returning to Salem entirely loaded with sugar. He later commanded the *America* on its first privateering cruise in 1812. On her next voyage under Captain Stephen Phillips, the *Recovery* went to Hamburg and thence to Calcutta. In 1801, having in the meantime been sold to Colonel Derby and now under command of Captain Luther Dana, she brought back from Mocha 326,000 lb. of coffee (and Captain Dana's manuscript sailing directions for the Mocha roads) to a group of four Salem merchants. The Salem ship *Ulyssees* was the next American vessel to call at Mocha. It was put about in Salem at the time, possibly by the owners, that the *Recovery* and the *Ulyssees* were the only American ships which the Imam of Yemen would admit to the Mocha roads. Unhappily the latter was wrecked off Cape Cod in February 1802.

In 1804 an American attempt was made to establish a factory at

B*

Mocha. Some of the American captains, amongst them Benjamin Crowninshield, Henry Elkins, Bancroft, Lee and Rowe, obtained the Governor of Mocha's permission to fly their flag on the house which they had hired in the town. They were nevertheless very unpopular with the English merchants at the port who considered that they were ruining the trade by paying high prices for coffee. Another matter which incurred the displeasure of the English was the Americans' insistence on jettisoning their ballast in the roads. Dr. Pringle, the English resident, complained of this to the Governor but seems to have obtained little redress. The Imam had not recognised the Americans as a nation at that time, but American merchants calling there had promised to bring presents to him from their government in the following year and then to establish a factory. The first American factory was built in the south-west quarter of Mocha. As the first decade of the nineteenth century progressed American activity at Mocha intensified. Captain Dutton Williams in command of the *Nancy* and William Leech with the *Suwarow* both put into Mauritius after successful visits to Mocha in October 1804. The next year, the *Cora* (Captain George Billfort) and the *Hebee* (Captain James Pearsall) visited the port. At the end of 1804 the *America* (Captain Benjamin Crowninshield), of ten guns, built by Beckett, was one of eleven ships from Salem and Baltimore lying at anchor in the Mocha roads. She had been sent by her owner, George Crowninshield, on July 2, 1804, on the first American voyage to Sumatra for pepper. At Mauritius on the return voyage her captain decided, against orders, to go to Mocha for coffee, and arrived there on December 1. At Mocha he picked up gum and hides, loading senna at both Aden and Mukulla before heading back home. The *Margaret*, built in Salem in 1800 by Beckett for John Derby and Benjamin Pickman, was at Mocha in 1804 under the command of Captain Henry Elkins: a distinguished ship, she had previously traded to Japan in 1801, under command of Captain Samuel Derby, the fourth American ship to do so. On May 25, 1805, probably bearing the promised presents for the Imam and the necessary authority and equipment to establish a factory, Captain Daniel Bray, Jnr. took the barque *Mary* out of Salem harbour bound for Mocha.

Navigational difficulties were perhaps the least of the hazards encountered at that time by ships in the Red Sea. The Salem ship

Essex, owned by William Orne (Captain Joseph Orne), with 60,000 dollars in specie on board, arrived in the Red Sea in 1806 bound for Hodeida. At Mocha the *Essex* augmented her crew with some thirty Arabs, but all of these turned out to be in the employ of a pirate, Muhamad Ikil, who beguiled Orne and his ship away to a point off Kamaran. Here the *Essex* was boarded, the crew murdered and the ship burned. The headless body of Orne and the mutilated remains of the merchants were washed ashore at Mocha, there to be buried in the Christian cemetery to the north of the town. The only survivor, a Dutch boy named John Herman Poll, was taken to Morebat in Dhofar by Muhamad Ikil as a slave. (The boy embraced Islam, married an Arab girl and was seen some years later by Lieutenant Charles Cruttenden of the Bombay Marine during his journey from Morebat to Salalah.) The news of the massacre reached Salem from Baltimore in October 1806 when a ship had arrived there from Mocha bearing the details of the story. However, two British ships, the *Mornington* and *Ternate*, were at Muscat at this time and Captain David Seton, the British Resident there, took the two vessels to Mocha to search for the pirates, without success. The *Essex* was not the only American vessel which met disaster on the Arabian coast at this period. The Boston ship *Commerce* (Captain Samuel Johnson of Rhode Island) was wrecked near Morebat in July 1792 and the survivors ill-treated on shore. Many of them, however, managed to make the overland journey to Muscat, whence they were shipped home.

In 1809, the year of Jefferson's Embargo Act, New York, Boston, Baltimore, Charleston and Portland were, in that order, the major trading ports of the east coast of America. Salem, although by New York standards a small port, had at that time 182 vessels in its overseas trading fleet. The Embargo Act, which allowed American ships to trade only with American ports, caused great hardship to Salem, Newburyport and Plymouth, and they never fully recovered their former prosperity. However, the *Margaret* managed to bring back a cargo of coffee from Mocha into Salem in October 1807, and with even greater enterprise the *Franklin* loaded 532,365 lb. the following year, delivering it to Joseph Peabody in Salem in December 1808. When the embargo was lifted in March 1809 oriental trade was immediately resumed and in that year two million pounds of coffee were imported from Mocha, the *America* making a substantial contribution to the total.

There was a further interruption of trade in 1812 when America declared war on Great Britain. When peace came in 1815, Salem's overseas trading fleet had dwindled to fifty-seven ships and the European carrying trade in which they had been able to take part during the previous years was now being taken up again by the maritime nations of Western Europe.

The Mocha trade was revived, however, with steady if infrequent visits, and in January 1819 there were four American ships loading coffee in the roads. The Salem brig *Java* (Captain William H. Neal) and another American vessel called at the port in 1822 and the brig *Beulah* (Captain Charles Forbes) opened the Madagascar trade in 1821 on her way home from Mocha. Captain Charles Millet commanded the Salem brig *Ann* which left Salem on March 12, 1826, bound for Zanzibar. Although she was one of the first American ships to call at the island, Captain Millet was unable to do any trading there and, hearing that Mocha was in a state of famine, he decided to employ his ship in taking food into the port. He arrived at Mocha on June 20, stayed there loading coffee until the beginning of 1827 and eventually arrived back at Salem having completed a most successful voyage. The *Black Warrior* (Captain John Bertram) was the first Salem ship to establish trade with Zanzibar. She brought back a large consignment of coffee from Mocha in 1832.

Salem made a final effort to revive her overseas trade, in spite of the fact that the harbour was becoming totally inadequate to cope with the rapidly expanding size of the new vessels, and so gained a temporary stay of execution. Joseph Peabody's Salem-built brig, the *Leander*, made twenty-six voyages to Europe, Africa and the Far East during the twenty-three years following 1821, and his ship *George* made twenty-one voyages to Calcutta between 1815 and 1837. Salem clung desperately to her specialities like the copal of Zanzibar. Salem owners were no longer prepared to arrange exclusive voyages to the Red Sea, but her ships bound for the Indian Ocean and East Africa were able to maintain an intermittent contact with Mocha. But the copal trade with Zanzibar was a poor substitute for the Calcutta, China and Sumatra voyages which had ended with Peabody's death.

(v) THE BRITISH IN ADEN 1839

American participation in the Mocha coffee trade had lasted barely half a century, but it was sufficient to influence British policy in South-west Arabia. The Americans having ousted the British from any substantial participation in the Mocha trade, Great Britain by 1837 was already turning her attention toward Aden. She had experienced constant difficulties with the Mocha authorities, and Aden, controlled by the Sultan of Lahej independently of the Yemen since 1728, appeared to be a more satisfactory trading station. Mocha at this time was almost at the end of a long period of decline. Captain S. B. Haines of the Indian Navy had reported favourably upon Aden as a harbour in 1835, and in 1837 Captain James MacKenzie of the Bengal Light Cavalry, who had called at Mocha, Jedda and Hodeida on his return journey to England from India, revealed in his report to the Foreign Office that Muhamad Ali was planning to capture Aden. Ever since 1832, Muhamad Ali had been consolidating his position in the Yemen, and by 1839 pressure was brought to bear by both Great Britain and Turkey for the evacuation of Muhamad Ali's forces from the Tihama. MacKenzie, however, had emphasised the need for a rapid British occupation not only to forestall the Egyptian Pasha but to obtain security of tenure of Aden as a commercial centre and as a refuelling station for the new steam vessels now plying between Suez and India.

Revival of interest in the development of the overland route between Alexandria and Suez or Kosseir, on the Egyptian Red Sea coast, was becoming apparent by 1820, and in the following ten years some primitive arrangements – felucca traffic or camels across the Nile Delta and horse or camel transport across the Egyptian deserts – were put in hand for the transportation of passengers and freight. The use of steam vessels after 1830 stimulated the progress of this overland route (Kosseir was finally abandoned as a pick-up point); the British and Indian governments now became involved in large-scale transportation of coal to the East. As early as 1828 a coaling station was established at Mocha and early in 1829 coal was dumped by the *Thetis* at Sirah Island, Aden, for the use in 1830 of the *Hugh Lindsay*, the first steamship to sail between India and Suez. Because of shortage of labour in Aden, the project to use Sirah as a coaling station was not a success and Mukulla was used temporarily for this purpose. Partly with the object of selecting suitable sites for coaling stations, Captain S. B. Haines was sent by the Bombay Government in 1834 to survey the Hadhramaut coast, while Socotra was also surveyed by him at this time. He returned to Bombay in command of the *Palinurus* and proceeded to Qishn in October of the same year on orders of the Bombay government to negotiate with the Sultan for the purchase of Socotra, which was a part of his territory. The outcome of the negotiations at Qishn were unsatisfactory but, in anticipation of success, the Bombay Government had already sent the *Tigris* (Commander R. Lowe), *Shannon* (Lieutenant Warry) and an armed *patteran* carrying two companies of native infantry, together with sappers and artillery all under Captains R. A. Bailey and Corsellis, to occupy the island. The troops stayed several months and the Sultan finally agreed to the landing of coal. In April 1835 the *Coote* (Captain Rose) relieved the *Tigris*, but fever had so reduced the garrison at Tamarida that it was shortly withdrawn.

Even when provided with a ready-made excuse for the British occupation of Aden, the Governor-General of India acted slowly. In January 1836 the *Deria Dowlat*, a Madras ship flying British colours and belonging to a niece of the Nawab of the Carnatic, was carrying a number of pilgrims bound for Mecca when she ran aground near Aden. The Arabs looted the vessel, and grossly maltreated the passengers and crew. Haines, who was at Mocha in command of the *Coote*, then sailed to Aden arriving on January 4, 1836. After he had demanded the return of the cargo or an indemnity of 12,000 Maria Theresa dollars, an attempt was made by henchmen of the local Sultan to capture him, but he escaped and returned to Bombay, having obtained an agreement from the Sultan of Lahej that Aden would be handed over to the British when troops arrived to occupy it. Haines, with Lieutenant Hamilton, was again off Aden in the *Coote* in September 1838 with Captain Denton and thirty European soldiers aboard, together with John Western of the Bombay Engineers who later planned the Aden fortifications. The Sultan refused to surrender the town and, when the *Mahi* and *Ann Crichton* arrived on January 11 the next year laden with coal for Sirah Island, a skirmish followed. Haines called for reinforcements and in response HMS *Volage* (Captain Smith) and HMS *Cruizer* (Lieutenant E. W. S. Daniell)

with 300 European and 400 Indian troops under Major Baillie
arrived on January 16, 1839. Three days later, Haines having
meanwhile taken the *Volage* and Smith the *Coote*, Aden was
taken by storm.

Haines became the first political agent and Lieutenant Jenkins
his first acting assistant. Jenkins however, was succeeded in
September 1840 by Lieutenant C. J. Cruttenden, one of Haines'
officers from the *Palinurus* days. Officers of the Indian Navy held
all the political appointments in Aden until 1855 when they were
replaced by army officers, Brigadier-General W. N. Coghlan
being the first such to be appointed political resident. Haines and
Cruttenden held office in Aden until 1854 when they were
replaced, a Commission of Inquiry having found a large deficit in
the public accounts.

British occupation of Aden produced some violent reactions
from the surrounding tribes. On November 11, 1839, the Abdali
Sultan tried unsuccessfully to retake Aden and two other abortive
attacks were made on May 21, 1840, and July 5, 1841, in an
attempt to oust the British from the town. After the attempt of
1841, the attacking force retired to Bir Ahmad, built a fort there
and began carrying out sporadic raids. The next year, after further
attacks, there was a severe struggle and two Arab forts on the
mainland were destroyed.

Meanwhile, on April 22, 1840, Ibrahim Pasha – whose Egyptian
forces had, the previous year, again been pressing south in
attempts to take possession of the fertile Hujariah area – withdrew
from Hodeida, which was occupied on the same day by the forces
of Hussein ibn-Ali ibn-Haidar to whom Ibrahim had ceded control.
Hussein, who in 1836 had been clerk to the Egyptian Governor at
Mocha, was now Sherif of Abu Arish, his forces on this occasion
being commanded by his brother, Abu Taleb. Muhamad ibn-Aun,
Sherif of Mecca, and the Imam of Sana had both been anxious to
gain control of the Tihama, but Ibrahim Pasha had considered
Hussein a more astute ruler. Muhamad Ali had negotiated with
the Imam offering to restore to him, on payment of a lakh of
rupees, the areas of the Tihama and the Yemen proper which had
now been taken by the Sherif of Abu Arish. The Imam, however,
had been unable to accept this offer because of the poor state of his
finances. Sheikh Ali Humeida of Bajil was also an unsuccessful
candidate for the control of the Tihama.

Muhamad Ali certainly wished ardently to take possession of Aden and he had, at least once, sent a mission to the Imam asking him to drive the British into the sea, but the Imam was adamant about the impossibility, for him, of effectively opposing Aden. Consequently, Ibrahim Pasha handed over the affairs of state to Hussein with the proviso that he paid an annual tribute to Constantinople; Haines sent a ship to Hodeida during the handover to protect British interests. Hussein, now in control of the Tihama (Zabid and Mocha had already been evacuated by the Egyptians) showed great hostility toward the British in Aden. The particular objects of this hostility were the British Vice-Consul and British subjects at Mocha. He had cut down the Union Jack flying in the town, and insulted Lieutenant Gordon and the captain of the Company's frigate *Zenobia* which had been sent to protect British subjects. Hussein arrogantly demanded the surrender of Aden, direct from the Bombay Government. The British protested to Constantinople, but with little effect. A local fanatic from Danwa, Al-Faqih Said, seized Taizz in October 1840, and proclaimed his divine mission of forcing the British out of Aden but he was killed two months later by the Imam's forces.

After Hodeida had been handed over to Hussein ibn Ali by the Egyptians, the Imam sent his nephew to Aden to protest against the handover and to ask the British for a treaty of friendship and trade. The next year he sent two missions to Aden to enlist British naval co-operation in his attempts to regain control of the Tihama from Hussein. The second mission, sent in July, was authorised to accept any conditions if Hussein could be defeated. After his third abortive request, in 1843, he abandoned hope of British help. This third mission had asked for a British officer to reside in Sana to act as adviser to the Imam: even this unique opportunity was refused by Haines and the offer was not repeated for more than a century. The Bombay Government had even refused to allow Cruttenden to go to Sana to persuade the Imam to keep his frontier north of Kataba in order to leave a buffer state between Aden town and the Imam's domains.

Both the Imam and Great Britain had referred the question of the control of the Tihama to Constantinople. The Turks replied by sending their representative Ashraf Bey to Zabid in September 1842 to negotiate with the interested parties but, after his arrival, he eluded Cruttenden who had been sent to meet him. The outcome of Ashraf's visit was that Hussein was made Pasha of the Tihama on consideration of a payment by him to Constantinople; Ashraf returned to the Tihama in 1847 to invest Hussein with Turkish insignia. In the early months of 1848, Bajil, Hodeida, Zabid, Beit al Faqih and Mocha were suddenly seized by the Imam, Muhamad Yahya, and Hussein was taken prisoner. Hussein, however, soon escaped, recaptured Zabid, and by treachery caused Mocha to be surrendered to him after two months' siege. Thus he regained control of the Tihama. In the same year, the Imam again wrote to Haines asking for his assistance and again had no success. In the meantime the Turkish government had started direct interference in south Arabian affairs. Hussein's hegemony was short-lived, for the Turks retook the Tihama when Tufiq Pasha's army seized Hodeida early in 1849 forcing Hussein to retire to Abu Arish. Tufiq Pasha himself became Governor of the Tihama and a treaty was soon drawn up at Hodeida in which it was agreed, among other things, that Sana was to be garrisoned with Turkish troops. The Imam returned from Hodeida to Sana with Tufiq Pasha and shortly afterwards the contents of the treaty were published. During the night following the announcement, most of the Turkish troops in the town were massacred by the Imam's men (the Imam's authority over Yemenis in the coastal areas was nominal) and Tufiq Pasha, badly wounded, only just managed, through bribery, to escape with a few of his soldiers but, completely exhausted by the journey, he died of wounds soon after his arrival at Hodeida.

(vi) FRENCH ACTIVITY 1820–70

In 1799 Napoleon had slipped back to France from Egypt, made himself First Consul, and won a series of victories in Italy, Prussia, Austria and Spain. For ten years up to 1809, his government in the Middle East was involved in an abortive series of intrigues with Persia with the object of mounting an overland invasion of India with Russian help. In 1810 the British took Mauritius and thus temporarily put an end to French power in the Indian Ocean. The difficulties of the Russian and Iberian Peninsula campaigns diverted so much French effort away from Egypt and the Red Sea that England was, for the time being, left undisputed master in the area. However, even as early as 1806, in spite of occasional reconnaissances, French ambitions were no longer seriously directed towards Egypt and her policy became one of strengthening the Ottoman Empire in order to deter a possible Russian occupation of Turkey; and as the century progressed France turned her attention towards consolidating her position in the Mediterranean and to taking an early part in the scramble for Africa. To this end she occupied Algeria in 1830, and began a few years earlier to reconnoitre the Red Sea with the particular object of opening up lasting commercial relations with Abyssinia and to a lesser extent with Arabia, where the Yemen was first to claim her attention. In 1823 one Bréon was sent there to collect specimens of the coffee tree in order to improve the strains of the berry being grown in the island of Réunion. In 1830 and 1831 another French botanist, Bové, travelled through the Hodeida area, while six years later a French doctor, Paul Emile Botta, in the service of Muhamad Ali, landed at Hodeida and journeyed through Beit al-Faqih and Hais to Taizz. Botta, a botanist of some repute, had been commissioned ostensibly by the Natural History Museum of Paris to explore the Yemen, but he was not able to reach Sana; however he managed – and this was a considerable achievement at that time – to climb Jebel Sabir near Taizz in the course of his researches, before travelling on to Mocha. Another French doctor in Muhamad Ali's service was Chedufau who, when an army under Ahmad Pasha, the Turkish Commander-in-Chief in the Yemen, was sent to restore order in Asir, accompanied the expedition as chief surgeon. Maurice Tamisier, arriving in Cairo late in 1833, managed to attach himself to the army as Chedufau's secretary, later discovering that two more of his countrymen, Planat and Mari, were also serving in Ahmad Pasha's force. The following year Victor Fontanier called at ports on both sides of the Red Sea, including Mocha, where he found a French East India Company ship in the roads. He published a detailed account of his observations which was later translated into English and published in London.

Mocha was visited in 1835 by several Frenchmen, among whom were Maurice Tamisier and Edouard Combes, who explored large areas of Abyssinia in that and the following year, and the brothers A. T. and Arnauld d'Abbadie. The reports of Combes and Tamisier inspired both a French Government expedition to the Red Sea coasts and to Abyssinia between 1839 and 1843 under Lieutenant Charlemagne Lefèbvre and the investigation of Mocha

by a young explorer and political intriguer, Charles Rochet
d'Héricourt, in 1839. Rochet d'Héricourt spent a long time in the
Shoa region of Abyssinia attempting to win over the King to the
side of France, but he was successfully countered by the efforts
of the more experienced J. Ludwig Krapf, a naturalised British
missionary, who had spent many years in Africa and the Red Sea.
A further result of Combes' and Tamisier's journeys was the
despatch of a 'scientific expedition' to Adowa in 1840 under two
officers of the French Army corps of engineers. Combes and
Tamisier set out from France on a second expedition in 1840, this
time backed by a French commercial house and supported by an
armed merchant ship, the *Ankobar*. The alarm felt in London at the
increasing intensity of French activity in the Red Sea caused
instructions to be sent to Haines in Aden to purchase some land
which would control the roadstead of Tajura. As a result Haines
sent Captain Robert Moresby in command of the *Sestrosis* with
the *Euphrates* (Lieutenant Barker) to enter into negotiations with
the local chiefs. Three small islands in and near the Bay of Tajura
and another controlling Zeila were bought for trifling sums to
neutralise the effect of the French purchase of the Edd roadstead,
farther north. But French activity continued and the arrival of
A. T. d'Abbadie in Aden in December 1840 led indirectly to a
British expedition to Shoa in 1841, with the aim of acquiring
territory and concluding a treaty, neither of which results was
achieved. In Shoa the French won more favour than the British.
The French corvette *Prévoyante* cruised in the Red Sea in 1838
under Captain Guillain, frequently calling at Mocha, and in the
winter of 1841 she took part in a French naval expedition along
the Red Sea Coasts. In Janury 1842 she anchored in the Mocha
roads and sent Ensign J. Passama ashore to make investigations.
Passama had a scientific bent, and as a result of his journeys to
Hais and Zabid he compiled a comprehensive topographical and
meteorological report. The French consul at Jedda at this period,
Fulgence Fresnel, was particularly active in his interest in the
Yemen; he also was an amateur scientist and received much
information from a French doctor T. J. F. Arnaud, who had been
in the Egyptian army, and who reached Sana in July 1843: after
visiting Marib, Arnaud sent Fresnel copies of a large number of
Himyaritic inscriptions which he had found in the ruins. Much
later Marib was visited again, by a French Jew disguised as a

Rabbi – Joseph Halevy. Halevy was comissioned by the French Academy of Inscriptions and the Alliance Israëlite Universelle to work in the Yemen, and he visited Sana and many other places in the territory in 1869 and 1870. Finally, in May 1887, the scientist Albert Deflers landed at Hodeida and travelled through Manakha to Sana, collecting botanical specimens. He penetrated into the remote areas of Kaukaban and Amran, north-west of Sana, and returned to the coast through Taizz, Zabid and Beil al-Faqih.

France had renewed her relations with Zanzibar in 1840 and occupied Nossi Bé, an island off Madagascar, in the following year. By now the steamship was a common sight in the Red Sea and Haines was constantly harassed by requests for coal from the captains of French ships. France's efforts were being directed to the purchase of one or more coaling stations, and her attempts to buy Ras Hafun (after surveying the Somali coast and Socotra) in 1847 and Kamaran Island in 1851 were rendered abortive by the interference of the Indian Navy. It was not until the arrival of an expedition under M. Schaeffer in 1862 that by purchasing Obok the French were able to lay firm foundations for the development of French Somaliland and the control of the outlet of Abyssinian trade at the port of Djibouti. By this time construction of the Suez Canal had already begun and France had thus assured herself of a ready-made coaling station at the entrance to the Red Sea. The French had been well aware of the increasing importance to them of the Red Sea from the earliest days of the Suez Canal project, and the British Government, foreseeing French intentions, issued orders in 1856 for the reoccupation of Perim and for the construction there of a lighthouse.

In December 1856 an American ship had brought news to Aden that a French brig, the *Narcisse*, was on its way from Zanzibar with specific orders to occupy Perim. The Resident at Aden, Brigadier-General Coghlan, had already received his orders from London to occupy the island and on January 11, 1857, just as the *Mahi* (Lieutenant C. B. Templer) was about to leave Aden with the occupation garrison under Lieutenant J. M. Greig and Lieutenant Billamore, the French ship arrived in Aden harbour. The Union Jack was hoisted over Perim on the following day and the garrison installed. The French, being thus frustrated, directed their energies elsewhere in the Red Sea, but in 1865 a French merchant M. Roubeau bought Sheikh Said from a local chief and built a factory there. But the factory soon fell into disuse and by 1870 it was abandoned, and the concession reverted to the French Government, which had obtained permission from Turkey in 1869 to establish a coaling station there. Due to British interference, the concession was held in abeyance and the coaling station project never materialised.

Thus, while for some forty years the British in Aden were kept continually on the alert by French intrigues in the Red Sea, both before and after the opening of the Suez Canal, the constant watchfulness by the Aden authorities and their ability to take counter-measures kept France's foothold in the Red Sea confined to Somaliland and thus at a respectful distance from Aden and the Yemen.

3

BEGINNINGS OF THE FRONTIER PROBLEM

(i) TURKISH TROOPS IN THE YEMEN

During the early years of the British occupation of Aden, the authorities were beset with problems arising from disturbances in the hinterland, and strong defensive measures were necessary. Sayed Ismail, a local religious leader, attacked the settlement and was driven off on August 17, 1846, but he attacked again nine days later and was routed with the help of the *Sesostris* (Lieutenant Hamilton) and some gunboats anchored near Khormaksar. In 1850 the crew of a boat from the *Auckland* was attacked while landing on the north shore of Aden Bay; one of the crew was killed and others were wounded. Many more atrocities were perpetrated during the following fifteen years. Captain Milne, a commissariat officer, was killed and others, including Lieutenant M'Pherson of the 78th Highlanders, were wounded in February 1851, when their shooting party was attacked by one of the Sayed community of Waht. Lieutenant Delisser, of the same regiment, was also attacked a few days later but he managed to kill his assailant with a knife. In July the *Sons of Commerce* was wrecked near Aden and her mate and a seaman murdered by members of the Abdali tribe. The instigator of the crime was sought out and executed by order of the Abdali Sultan, who continued for a time to remain on friendly terms with the Aden authorities. At the end of 1857 the British payment of a stipend to the Abdali Sultan was stopped because his men had been plundering merchandise coming into Aden from Bir Ahmad. To retaliate, the Sultan, Ali, immediately stopped sending supplies into Aden and occupied Sheikh Othman. A punitive expedition from Aden then set out under Brigadier-General Coghlan with a detachment from the *Elphinstone* and, having captured Sheikh Othman, blew up the fort and the village. At the end of 1865 Colonel Woolcombe, at the head of 500 troops and accompanied by the Resident, Sir William Merewether, brought the Fadhli Sultan to submission, after the Fadhli tribe had looted caravans going into Aden, and in May 1867 the Sultan pledged himself to stop any more raiding and to keep the peace within his area.

For the next nine years there was comparative peace, the Abdali Sultan eventually coming to terms with the Resident. After the defeat of Tufiq Pasha's expedition to Sana in 1849 the Turks managed to retain their foothold on the coast of the Yemen; however the interior relapsed into anarchy, nine Imams trying to rule the high plateaux during the following six years. The opening of the Suez Canal in 1869 finally stirred the Turks into action, and troops under Raouf Pasha were sent to the Yemen. Raouf Pasha fell ill and in April 1871 a new expeditionary force under Mukhtar Pasha reoccupied Sana and most of the towns of the Yemen were garrisoned by Turkish troops. As soon as they had consolidated their position the Turks proceeded to harass the British in Aden and, having urged and assisted the tribes in the southern Yemen to take Lajeh, encroached into the Abdali, Haushabi and Amiri countries and finally occupied Dhala. This attempt at encirclement prompted Colonel J. W. Schneider, the Resident, to march to Lahej with a small force, and the Turks withdrew, despite the appearance in Aden harbour of two Turkish warships with 1,200 troops aboard. The arrival on the scene of HMS *Wolverine* shortly afterwards soon made the Turkish ships put to sea.

The early Zeidi Imams were defeated by the Rasulid dynasty in the thirteenth century and remained in relative obscurity until the Turkish occupation of the Yemen some 300 years later when they again emerged as spiritual rulers of the country. In about 1868 was born one who probably held the Imamate for the longest period, Yahya ibn-Muhamad. His grandfather, Yahya Hamid al-Din, led a revolt against Turkish rule and oppression in 1891, and besieged Sana for many weeks: his force was only dispersed in 1892, after much bloodshed, by the Turkish general Ahmad Feizi Pasha who landed at Hodeida and, burning 300 villages as he went, fought his way through the mountains to relieve the capital. Husein Hilmi Pasha took the place of Yahya Hamid al-Din in 1897 and, although progressive, he in turn was displaced by Abdullah Pasha in 1900. Muhamad Ali Mansur soon succeeded, but he died in 1904 and his place was taken by his son Yahya ibn-Muhamad. Quickly advancing south from Sada at the head of his followers Imam Yahya took possession of Sana and proceeded to spread his rule over the highlands. Ahmad Feizi Pasha, then filling a post in Baghdad, was ordered to make a rapid journey across Arabia to Yenbo, and to take ship to Hodeida to command another expeditionary force which had been assembled there. Fighting his way through the mountains, he retook Sana in September 1905, afterward maintaining his garrisons in the capital and some other principal towns. Hassan Tahsin Pasha was appointed Governor General in 1908 and made many concessions to Imam Yahya, including the administration of the religious law and the Islamic taxation system; relations between the Turks and the Imam thereafter improved beyond all recognition. The next Governor-General, Muhamad Ali Pasha, who took office in 1910, was less successful. Imam Yahya again marched on Sana, this time with 150,000 men. He besieged the town for three months until yet another Turkish expeditionary force, this time under Izzet Pasha, came to its relief. Izzet Pasha eventually found means of coming to terms with Imam Yahya and, with the Italians now at war with Turkey and bombarding the Yemeni ports, a compromise in the administration of the country was agreed upon. Eventually, in 1913, a proclamation was made from Constantinople announcing an *entente* between the Turks and the Imam who, in addition to receiving a handsome subsidy, retired to Shahara in the north from where he was allowed to appoint certain provincial governors and to administer the traditional Islamic legal code. The years of bloodshed had come to an end and the Imam Yahya was not again to emerge as a potent factor in South West Arabian affairs until 1919.

(ii) THE ANGLO–TURKISH BOUNDARY COMMISSION 1902–4

As early as 1892, General Jopp, the Political Resident, made arrangements for surveying the tribal areas between the Yemen and Aden, and Captain Wahab (later Wauhope) and Captain Domville spent some time up country carrying out the survey. The project eventually had to be abandoned because of local hostility, and little more was done to survey the borderlands until 1902. In 1900 Muhamad Nasir Muqbil, of the Humar tribe, had erected a tower in Haushabi territory at Kafuf, two miles northwest of Al-Darejh, in order to divert the caravan traffic through his own hands and thus increase his income and prestige. In July a small body of troops under the command of Major

Rowe of the Royal West Kent Regiment went to assist the Haushabi in ejecting the Humar from the tower. Meanwhile, Muqbil had informed the Turks at Taizz that the object of the British expedition was to acquire Turkish territory. The Turks' reaction was swift, and they sent 400 men to occupy the tower at Kafuf. The Humar were routed from the heights near Al-Darejh by Major Rowe's force, and the column then attacked the tower before sunset. The Turks, unable to withstand this onslaught, evacuated the tower during the night. This setback was too much for the Ottoman Government which, reversing its current policy, suggested a demarcation of the Aden–Yemen frontier.

As a result, an Anglo–Turkish Boundary Commission, which was appointed in November 1901, first met early in the next year, and continued its existence until May 23, 1904. In January 1902, escorted by two companies of Indian infantry, the British members of the Boundary Commission, Colonel Wahab and Mr. Fitzmaurice, proceeded to Dhala to join the Turkish members, who arrived soon afterwards, but local disorders at Bal Haf made it necessary for Wahab to send an expedition there from Dhala to destroy a fort. Throughout the first year of the Commission's existence, the Turks remained obstructive and by the beginning of 1903 no progress had been made. The Turks continued to occupy Jalilah. In March 1903 a British force of 2,200 men was assembled at Dhala; a mountain battery was soon dispatched there as a reinforcement and two Royal Naval cruisers of the Mediterranean Fleet were standing to in Aden harbour. British and Indian infantry also occupied Dar Aggan, but at the end of March the Turks evacuated Jalilah and retired to Kataba, the British Commissioners following to Sana where they remained until the end of 1903. The Boundary Commission was able, at the beginning of February 1904, to enter Subeihi territory, and during April all British troops returned to Aden with the exception of a wing of the 9th Russell's Infantry, which remained to support the Commission; a strong garrison was also left at Dhala with Major Merewether, the recently appointed Political Officer. On May 23 the Commission at last returned with its escort to Aden and adjourned to Perim to complete its work. In November Lieutenant-Colonel H. F. Jacob succeeded Major Merewether at Dhala and remained in that post until the evacuation of the hinterland in September 1907. A 150-mile boundary line was laid down by the

Anglo–Turkish Commission between Bab el-Mandeb and Wadi Bana, and this was scrupulously observed by the Turks until their influence in the Yemen began to wane and the Imam began moving over the border in 1907. The deliberations on the frontier question were eventually incorporated in an agreement signed in April 1909, and in the Anglo–Turkish Convention of 1914.

(iii) THE FIRST WORLD WAR

Soon after the outbreak of war in 1914 the Turkish 7th Yemen Army Corps, under the command of the Circassian officer, Ali Said Pasha, could muster some 14,000 troops in thirty-five battalions, many of whom had already seen service in Syria. The 39th Division was stationed at Sana and the 40th at Hodeida. The 21st and 22nd (independent) Divisions, the latter commanded by Ghaleb Pasha, had their headquarters respectively at Loheia and Mecca, and when the Turks attacked at Lahej in 1915, 2,000 Turkish troops, 4,000 Yemenis and ten cannon were in the field. The latter contingent consisted of about 3,000 Arab levies, some Subeihi and Yafei and all the Haushabi of Hujariah. Against this was the tiny Aden garrison – one British and one Indian infantry battalion and the Aden Troop of Indian cavalry some 100 strong. It was not surprising therefore that the Turks soon began to invest Aden and to march to the extreme south-west of the British sphere; but Brigadier-General H. V. Cox with the 29th Indian Infantry Brigade was soon on the scene and, under cover of the guns of a Royal Naval cruiser he landed at Sheikh Said on November 9, 1914, to drive off a large force of Turks who were threatening Perim. His brigade was part of a considerable body of troops. Escorted by the *Duke of Edinburgh* (Captain Henry Blackett), *Swiftsure* and *Northbrooke* (an auxiliary cruiser of the Royal Indian Marine), a large convoy carrying five infantry brigades and the Imperial Service Cavalry Brigade had left India on November 2 en route for Egypt and France. Approval was sought and received from England to use some of these troops to remove the Turks from Sheikh Said, but the approval was given only on condition that the convoy was not delayed more than twenty-four hours. By November 8, the convoy was approaching Aden and as it did so the *Duke of Edinburgh*, in company with three transports including the *City of Manchester*, was sent ahead at full speed and at dawn on November 9 bombarded Fort Turba. As no reply came from the shore, Captain Blackett led in the transports and a landing was made – in face of sudden and considerable opposition. Early in the afternoon, half of the British troops had gone ashore and were advancing to clear the Turks from the remains of the fort. As the final assault on Fort Turba began, the Turks withdrew, and by nightfall all the surrounding hills were in British hands. The next morning Captain Blackett landed a demolition party and completely destroyed the fort. By six o'clock in the evening all troops had re-embarked and were proceeding up the Red Sea, Brigadier-General Cox leaving behind him at Aden the 23rd Sikh Pioneers who were later used to supplement the small garrison at Perim.

On the opposite coast of Arabia, at Muscat, the 95th Infantry and the 102nd Bombay Grenadiers had been successfully carrying out their garrison duties in the early months of 1915, but it was decided to reinforce them with half of the 126th Baluchistan Infantry. The other half of this force was sent to Aden when the 30th Indian Infantry Brigade to which it belonged was en route from Egypt to reinforce British troops in Mesopatamia. At the beginning of June 1915, the Aden garrison was weakened by the detachment of troops to Kamaran, the Farsans and other Red Sea islands, and as a Turkish advance on Aden seemed imminent a small mobile unit, known as the Aden Movable Column, was formed in the town from the limited resources available. In the meantime the Turks had reoccupied Sheikh Said and on June 13, 1915, they shelled Perim. The 23rd Sikh Pioneers withstood the Turkish attack on Perim which followed next day, and inflicted some casualties. (When Raouf Bey, commanding the brigade stationed near Sheikh Said, refused to attack Perim, Hafat Bey replaced him and he was sent in disgrace to Taizz.) Nevertheless, while the British were successful at Perim, Major-General D. L. B. Shaw, the military commander, had found it necessary to send the Aden Troop of cavalry to Lahej to assist the Abdali Sultan whose small garrison was all but wiped out by the Turks; the troop reached Nobat Dukaim but suffered the fate of the Sultan's forces. On July 3 the Aden Movable Column, now reduced to 1,000 men, set out to support them, but four Turkish battalions under Raouf Bey (now commanding the 115th Brigade) and Husni Bey, advancing from Mawiyah and Hujariyah, overcame the Abdali Sultan's forces at Tanan and Nobat Dukaim, and captured Lahej on July 5. One battalion of the Turkish 115th Brigade was left at Nobat and another at Zaida. The forces under British command, which had been handicapped by mutiny and desertion, were thus forced to retire on Bir Nasir, taking with them about forty Turkish prisoners. The exhausted remains of the British force reached Sheikh Othman at 9 a.m. on July 7; however, after refitting at Khormaksar they were able a fortnight later to force the Turks out of Sheikh Othman, which they had occupied in the meantime. The Abdali Sultan who had been accidentally shot by British troops, was taken by car to Aden, where he died from his wound under an operation. Aden was in such a desperate plight at this time that the authorities attempted to obtain the services of 800 French soldiers en route from Madagascar in a Messageries Maritime vessel which had called at Aden; in this they were unsuccessful.

The success at Sheikh Othman had been made possible by the arrival in Aden on July 8 of the 108th Infantry from India and, ten days later, of the 28th Frontier Force Brigade under Major-General Sir George Younghusband. After the victory of the 23rd Sikh Pioneers at Perim on June 14, 1915, it was proposed that Younghusband should take a brigade from Egypt to rout the Turks once more from Sheikh Said. Lord Kitchener, the Secretary of State for War, did not take kindly to the idea. On June 22 he signalled to Major-General Maxwell: 'Could we in a week capture the Turkish works and capture the guns which shell Perim? Could we withdraw our force when landed? We do not want to fritter away and diminish the strength of Egypt . . . Could adequate results be obtained by naval means only? We await the views of the Naval authorities.' However, when Younghusband landed a month later, he soon decided not to attempt to take Sheikh Said or Lahej but to consolidate his position in the Aden peninsula and fortify Sheikh Othman. Consequently, until the end of the war only sporadic fighting of a defensive character against the Turks was possible. In August and September 1915, Al Waht and Fiyush were taken from the Turks, who retired on Lahej. On September 10 Younghusband left Aden with the 28th Brigade, being relieved by Brigadier-General Price, who was then invalided in July 1916 and replaced in command by Major-General Sir James Stewart. In January 1916 troops from Aden had attacked Hatum but did not take the village until December 7, when Jabir was also occupied.

The Imam made a truce in November 1915 with the Idrisi who were outside his territory to the north, on the Red Sea coast, and were frequently skirmishing on the border, and Lieutenant-Colonel Jacob, who had continually worked to win over the Imam to the British cause, obtained a letter from him which indicated that while maintaining his allegiance to the Turks, he promised a favourable attitude toward Great Britain. Muhamad Yahya Sharif al-Din, the chief of the dynasty rivalling that of the ruling Imam, founded at this time the 'League of Ulema and Sharufa' with the object of expelling the Turks from the Yemen, and on April 27, 1916, the League wrote to the Aden Government offering its help against the Turks in exchange for money and munitions. The offer was declined.

During his term as GOC, Brigadier-General Price had considered that a show of force would impress the local tribesmen whom the Turks were attempting to rally to their assistance. He felt that such a demonstration could be achieved economically by the use of aircraft, and that such action would go a long way toward removing the threat to Aden. Thus, in February 1916, he urged his superiors in Egypt to send him what aircraft they could spare and by March 29 the *Raven II* (formerly the *Rabenfels* a German cargo ship) was steaming down the Red Sea, having received on board one Short and five Sopwith Schneider seaplanes from the *Ben-my-Chree*, which happened to be refitting at that time at Port Said. The *Raven II* hove to off Perim, erected her seaplanes and entered Aden harbour under cover of darkness on March 30.

A conference was convened by the GOC Aden at which the Commander-in-Chief of the East Indies Fleet and Flight Commander C. H. K. Edmonds, RNAS (in command of the six aircraft) were present. It was decided that a reconnaissance flight should be made on April 1 and, on the following three days, 20-lb. bombs were to be dropped on the Turkish camps near Waht, Fiyush and Subar. These decisions were carried out according to plan and, in addition, pamphlets were dropped in areas where tribesmen supporting the Turks were concentrated, urging them to desert from the Turkish troops. Unfortunately the naval authorities were pressing for the return of the *Raven II* and after only three days at Aden, she set sail up the Red Sea for Port Said.

The Shorts eaplanes returned two months later, this time

aboard the seaplane carrier *Ben-my-Chree*. As the carrier approached Aden at daybreak on June 7 aircraft were sent to reconnoitre the Lahej area only to discover that there were several Turkish camps north of Lahej and that at the camp near Subar there was also a sizeable depot. Other camps and gun positions were also noted. During the period June 7–12 low-level bombing attacks were made on the Turkish positions on the morning and evening of each day. In these operations larger bombs were used than previously, and a primitive petrol bomb was successfully dropped on the depot near Subar just before the *Ben-my-Chree* left Aden in the late afternoon of June 12. By dawn on June 13 the carrier was off Perim and from there her seaplanes bombed enemy camps at Jebel Malu and Jebel Akrabi. On that day also a Sopwith seaplane was used to spot for the *Ben-my-Chree*'s guns, which shelled the two camps.

No Germans are known to have taken part in the fighting between the Turks in Yemen and the British in Aden during the 1914–18 War. Some forty Germans did, however, land at Hodeida from Massawa in 1914 but at that time there appeared little prospect of their going into action on the side of the Turks and they therefore left the port. In the spring of 1916, a picked Turkish and Syrian force of 3,500, including an artillery battery and two machine gun companies, from the 29th Division at Constantinople all under command of Khairi Bey, arrived at Medina from Damascus by rail en route to the Yemen to reinforce Ali Said Pasha's two divisions. Twenty-four lieutenants for the force were to be supplied from the 128th, 129th and 130th Regiments of the 22nd Division. A German mission of three officers, two NCOs and two privates under Major Othman von Stötzingen had made its way from Damascus to Yanbo by June 1916, and was to have rejoined Khairi Bey's force at Qunfida and marched with it to augment the 7th Yemen Army Corps. The beginning of the Arab revolt on June 5 thwarted these plans, however, and the mission was captured by Amir Abdullah. The Turkish troops were absorbed into the Medina garrison and von Stötzingen returned from Yanbo to Damascus. It is probable that the denial of these reinforcements to the Yemen saved the Idrisi from annihilation, besides preventing material assistance being given to Mad Mullah, a religious leader in Somaliland, who was revolting against British rule, and had designs on Eritrea. If, in retrospect, the Arab revolt had nothing else to justify it, it may have prevented the Turks and Germans from taking Aden, which alone would have been fair reward for British-sponsored operations in the Hejaz.

The adventures in the Yemen of another German party under Kapitanleutnant von Mucke belong rather to the history of World War I than to that of foreign penetration of the country. The *Emden* was one of three fast light German cruisers based at Tsing-Tao in China which operated alone in Far Eastern waters. In addition to bombarding Madras on September 22, 1914, these cruisers had sunk a great tonnage of British shipping. The *Emden* was eventually sunk off the Keeling Islands by HMAS *Sidney*, while a landing party from the German cruiser was ashore at Direction Island, destroying a British telegraph station. The party, which consisted of three officers, six NCO's and forty matelots under von Mucke, an officer of great resource, was consequently stranded, but they managed to arm a small 97-ton schooner, the *Ayesha*, which they had found abandoned there. In this vessel they sailed for Padang where they beached her; there they took over a German ship, the *Choising* of 1,700 tons, and changed her name to *Chenir* making her out to be an Italian ship from Genoa. Von Mucke decided to make for Hodeida. Arriving in the straits of Bab-el-Mandeb on January 7, 1915, the *Choising* anchored off Hodeida unobserved by the Red Sea Patrols of Admiral Wemyss and on Janurary 9, von Mucke was conferring with Ghaleb Bey, commander of the Turkish 40th Division at Hodeida about the best way for himself and his party to return to Germany. Von Mucke and his men then made their way by caravan to Sana where, after staying a month, he decided that the difficulty of travelling northward was too great. So, returning to Hodeida, they embarked in two *sambuqs* at Jebhane inlet and sailed to Lith under cover of the coral banks. After many adventures the party, much reduced in numbers, finally made its way to the Hejaz railway at El Ala and thence travelled on to Damascus, and so to Constantinople.

(iv) THE FIRST WORLD WAR—*Continued*

The British had opened negotiations with the Idrisi in order to help them in harrying the Turks in the northern Yemen. The commander of the East Indies Squadron in the Red Sea, Vice-

Admiral Sir Robert Wemyss, decided to give the Idrisi any possible assistance in their efforts to drive the Turks from Loheia. Loheia had already been bombarded by the Royal Navy and attacked by the Idrisi in June 1915; the first Idrisi attack was unsuccessful but the Turkish surrender of the town was secured when, on February 18, 1917, the auxiliary cruiser HMS *Fox* appeared in the roads. However, it was not possible to conclude a treaty with the Idrisi until the following April.

Land-based aircraft were first used in action in South-west Arabia in December 1917. When the 7th Rajputs were fighting a stiff rearguard action through the scrub at Darab, the Turks were kept at bay with the help of the Royal Flying Corps in the role of artillery co-operation. In addition the RFC were employed in bombing Turkish camps up country. The Royal Naval Air Service was again in action in February 1918. The seaplane carrier *City of Oxford*, when off Loheia on February 22, sent up aircraft to reconnoitre and photograph Turkish positions at Jebel el-Mihl and Zohra. These positions were bombed for several days on end, with such effect that by February 28 the Idrisi were able to gain a footing in the hills. The Turkish headquarters at Zohra was also bombed at the request of the Idrisi in order to impress the local Yemeni tribes, many of whom deserted their Turkish leaders and went over to the Idrisi. On March 19 the *City of Oxford* steamed north to Maidi and her aircraft carried out demonstration flights over the town and over Wadi Habil. Bombing attacks were also made on the Turkish positions at Jebel el-Mihl and by March 22 the seaplane carrier was back off Loheia where further demonstration flights were made.

A visitor to Loheia in 1921 – Amin Rihani, an American–Syrian – wrote in his diary:

Loheia we found still suffering from the effects of Italian and English shells. It was bombarded twice, once by Italians and once by the British. . . . Loheia was held by the Turks until the last year of the World War and it was subject to bombardment by both sea and land. About two thousand Idrisi soldiers under the command of a British officer had occupied Abu Halaq which is five miles south of the town whilst a handful of Turks were holding the wells five miles east of it. The Idrisi expedition of which Dr. Fadl'ud-Din was the Medical Officer received water as well as ammunition from the British ships and Loheia after a double attack by land and sea was forced to surrender. Very soon after that, it received news of the Armistice. . . . The Naval officers came on land to celebrate with the Army officers the end of the war. . . .

Even the tiny coastal village of Salif was to play its small part in the war. It had been decided by the Muslim hierarchy in Mecca that the Pilgrimage, suspended since the war, should be reintroduced. Kamaran Island, the quarantine station for all northbound pilgrim ships, which had been occupied by the Royal Navy since 1915, was only accessible through a very narrow channel flanked on the east by the minute port of Salif, where a small Turkish detachment with two mountain guns was stationed; but this force was sufficient to constitute a threat to pilgrim shipping. Admiral Wemyss ordered the port to be captured and during the engagement ninety-three Turks were taken prisoner (including eight wounded) and six were killed, compared with two British wounded and four killed.

At the beginning of the war the Turks had interned about 200 British Indian subjects, detained them at Hodeida and meted out to them some unduly harsh treatment. The Indian Government having refused Admiral Wemyss' request to use the naval garrison on Kamaran to make a landing there, Captain Boyle, Senior Naval Officer Red Sea, was ordered to try to rescue the British internees. Captain Boyle's ultimatum was rejected and he proceeded to shell the Turkish public buildings near the town; but artillery replied from the shore and, being unable to affect a landing, Boyle proceeded to blockade the port. A number of Englishmen employed at the salt works at Salif before the War had also been taken to Sana and interned in 1914. As Dr. Richardson, the British Vice-Consul at Hodeida, was taken to Sana under escort in 1915 and M. Roux, the French Vice-Consul, was also interned in the capital, the French Government decided to send the *Desaix* (Capitaine de Vaisseau Vergos) to negotiate with the Turks for their release.

The World War at an end, the Imam with foresight soon began to sue for an alliance with Aden and, in addition to asking for munitions, notably quick-firing guns (and the men to operate them), he also sought British recognition of his sovereignty over the country between Ras Hali and the Hadhramaut with the

C

exception of Aden and the hinterland. These proposals were not favoured by the Idrisi with whom the British had made a treaty in April 1915, and were therefore not accepted by the British Government; this refusal, however, did not deter Lieutenant-Colonel Jacob (see page 43), from continuing his efforts to develop friendly relations with the Imam of whom he was always a champion. In December 1918, after a year of little military activity, the Turks, who refused to recognise the Armistice, continued to hold Lahej. The Movable Column from Aden was sent against them, and by the middle of December the Turkish forces surrounding Lahej had laid down their arms and Ali Said Pasha, an honourable soldier in defeat, marched into Aden with 1,000 men to hand over his sword. However, a Turkish officer and about 800 men had taken most of the Turkish arms and ammunition to Sana, where he remained on the Imam's staff. Sheikh Mohammed bin Ali of the Idrisi disarmed the Turks left in his area and sent them by *sambuq* to Kamaran when British steamships took them to Egypt. A Turkish captain and about sixty soldiers elected to remain in Asir and to enter the service of the Sheikh. In mid-December HMS *Juno* (Captain Alexander R. Palmer) HMS *Proserpine* (Commander Harold R. Bedwell) and an armed merchant cruiser, the *Suva* (Captain H. Buchanan-Wollaston), were off Hodeida, and bombarded the town in order to cover the landing of the 2nd/101st Grenadiers, who forced the surrender of the Turkish garrison. Aboard one of the naval vessels the former Vice-Consul, Dr. Richardson, was assisting in directing the fire. The garrison commander, Kaimakam Ghaleb Bey, commanding the 40th Division, escaped capture and went over to the Imam, and already at Sana the Turkish commander of artillery, several other officers and 300 men had entered the Imam's service along with the Governor-General, Mahmoud Nadim Bey.

(v) MAHMOUD NADIM BEY

Continuity in the administration of the Yemen during a great part of the first quarter of the twentieth century was provided by Mahmoud Nadim Bey. He had already been in the country for some years before the war, having succeeded Izzet Pasha as Governor-General of the Yemen in 1912, after the 1911 revolt. He was a dark, heavy-jowled and portly Syrian, wore high jackboots, and large gold rings on his fingers, and was never without one of his extra large Turkish cigarettes. In later years he took to wearing, occasionally, a *keffiyah* instead of the tarboush of the Turkish official in order to identify himself more closely with the Arabs. A tall, powerfully-built man, he seems to have grown fat during his long period of service in the Yemen: an early photograph shows him smart and slim in the black-braided uniform of a senior Turkish administrator; his moustaches were large even for those days.

During 1914-15, he was feverishly active in trying to win over the Idrisi Sheikh in Asir to the Turkish cause. The task was a difficult one and called for very careful management on his part. During World War I the continuance of good relations between the Turks and the Imam was solely due to his good offices, and during that time he issued a great deal of hostile propaganda against the British in Aden. When the war came to an end, and Ali Said Pasha surrendered in Aden, Mahmoud Nadim Bey remained in his palace at Sana, and it was he who handed over the reins of power to the Imam in 1919.

When Lieutenant-Colonel Jacob's mission was detained at Bajil by the Quhra sheiks in 1919, it was Nadim Bey who was deputed by the Imam to negotiate for its release with a ransom of 4,000 Turkish pounds. Frank and vehement in his views on the administration of the Yemen he realised how turbulent were the inhabitants of this poor relation of the Turkish imperial domains and the great extent to which they pursued their grievances. Before 1919, the majority of the officials were Arabs and he blamed them for much of the unrest, although he admitted that the Turks had maladministered the Yemen as much as other provinces. In 1919, in his new position as Adviser to the Imam, he said on one occasion: 'If I were still in power I would chastise these Arab dogs as in the olden days.' In reality, although he firmly believed that there would never be complete unity of the Arab peoples, he loved the Yemenis and earnestly hoped for an improvement in their condition. Latterly the Imam paid him scant courtesy. He was not the only former member of the Ottoman Government living in the Yemen after World War I, and he was ably assisted by a Turkish officer, his ADC, who was allowed to retain his *kalpak* and Turkish military uniform. Nadim was a strong character, frank and good company and always anxious to please Europeans

with whom he came into contact. He was never invested with the
dignity of Pasha, but from 1912 onwards was accorded the rank
as a courtesy. He finally returned to Syria in 1924 after twenty
years' continuous service in the Yemen.

(vi) BRITAIN AND IMAM YAHYA

Under the terms of the Armistice of Mudros of November 1918,
the Turks during March 1919 completely evacuated the Yemen
and later, under the Treaty of Lausanne of 1923, formally
renounced all their possessions in Arabia. The Idrisi had made
some territorial gains as a result of the war, but the Imam Yahya
now emerged as undisputed master of the Yemeni highlands, and
he was not inclined to follow the Turks into defeat. Although, as
de facto head of a successor state to Turkish Yemen, he should
have bound himself by Turkey's pre-war treaties, he never in
fact recognised the validity of the Anglo–Turkish Boundary
Commission of 1902–5 or of the Anglo–Turkish Convention of
1914. He was therefore now poised to harry the British in Aden
and to begin doing what the Turks had done, namely to threaten
all commercial intercourse between Aden and his own territory.

Although in theory the British had gradually strengthened their
position over the years, their position in the Aden hinterland was
insecure. Popham's treaty of 1802 had long been forgotten by the
time that Haines made a formal agreement with the Sultan of
Lahej in 1839. Turkish presence in the Yemen prompted the
signature, during the 26 years following 1871, of no fewer than
14 'treaties of protection'; the activities and military operations in
support of the Anglo–Turkish Boundary Commission gave rise
to 13 more and a further three were signed between 1912 and
1915, following the Italo-Turkish war. In 1919, thirty-one
'treaty chiefs' existed in the Aden hinterland and neighbouring
islands. Agreements with each chief followed similar lines, the
British extending their protection to the territory in question, and
the ruler promising not to enter into any relations whatever with
foreign governments other than the British, nor to sell or hire any
part of his domains to another power. Each agreement was sealed
with a reasonable subsidy, the continuance of which was dependent
upon the 'good behaviour' of the chief and his subjects. Haines,
during his fifteen years in Aden, had foreseen the need to create a

buffer between Aden and the Yemen and to this end he concluded agreements, which were not formal protection treaties as we now know them, with the Aqrabi, Fadhli, Haushabi, Subeihi and Lower Yafei rulers. In 1919 the protectorate treaties had the same aim – to create behind Aden an area free from interference from any foreign government. Perim was occupied under the eyes of the French in 1857, the Kuria Muria Islands had been given to the British by the Sultan of Oman in 1854, but Kamaran, formally disclaimed by Turkey in 1923, remained with an officially undetermined status. Great Britain's ascendancy over Mukulla and Socotra had been established long before the close of the nineteenth century and she had become entrenched, in varying degrees, at Berbera, Port Sudan and Suakin during the early years of the twentieth. In 1919 her immediate problem in Aden was to come to terms with Imam Yahya.

4

ANGLO-YEMENI RELATIONS BETWEEN
TWO WORLD WARS

(i) THE JACOB MISSION, 1919

The port of Salif, which in 1919 was occupied by a small British garrison, was handed over after a short time to the Idrisi together with the rest of the Tihama as far as and including Hodeida (also garrisoned with British troops). The Idrisi renounced all rights to Qunfida in favour of the protégés of King Husein of the Hejaz. The Imam very quickly took the opportunity to protest to the Resident at Aden about the British occupation of Hodeida, but the reply from Aden told him that the British troops were stationed there to maintain law and order and that control of the town would shortly be placed in the Imam's hands. Notwithstanding this assurance, the garrison remained, and Hodeida was handed over to the Idrisi in January 1921 when the Wazir of Asir entered the town at the head of a regiment of his troops. In the meantime the Aden authorities kept a political officer there (Dr. Muhamad Fadl' al-Din); they closed the town to the hinterland, and the Imam did not in fact obtain possession of Hodeida until April 1925, when it was ceded to him by Seyid Ali ibn Muhamad, the Idrisi Sheikh, and taken by his second son, Seif al-Islam Ahmad. A revolt against Seyid Ali had broken out in the town in 1924, and the Imam lost no time in obtaining a hold in it without bloodshed and with the concurrence of the inhabitants. This acquisition of the best outlet to the Red Sea from the highlands was a great advantage to the Imam, as the caravan trade had become increasingly difficult in recent years. Bajil had already fallen into the Imam's hands and, elated by their success, his forces advanced northward and took possession of Loheia and Maidi, forcing Seyid Ali ibn Muhamad to leave his territory and take refuge in Aden. Shortly afterwards Hassan bin Ali, Seyid Ali's uncle, who was living in Aden, landed without any warning at Jizan, rallied the populace and called upon Ibn Saud for assistance. This led Imam Yahya to negotiate with Hassan bin Ali and to recognise

Hassan's sovereignty over southern Asir (with his capital at Abu Arish) down to a point just north of Maidi.

Immediately after the Turkish departure in 1919 the Imam blocked the road to Dhala, thus halting for a time British intentions of regaining the old frontier of 1904; in an effort to promote some friendship with him, a mission under Lieutenant-Colonel H. F. Jacob set out from Cairo with the object of discussing with the Imam at Sana the future of the Yemen after the Turkish surrender. Lieutenant-Colonel Jacob took with him Major (now Sir) Bernard Reilly, Captain Richardson and Captain Brock of the RAMC, Jacob's Indian Secretary and al-Mughaira who was a member of the Pan-Arab party from Cairo. The mission, which was escorted by twenty-five men of the Aden Troop and a team of muleteers, arrived at Hodeida on August 18, 1919, and reached Bajil the next evening, where it was taken prisoner by Sheikh Abu Hadi of the Quhra tribe. The interventions of the Imam, who sent 130 soldiers under Mahmoud Nadim Bey to meet the mission with a ransom of £4,000 Turkish, and of the British who proffered £50,000 for its release, were of no avail. On September 30, the Royal Air Force commander at Aden received a request for aircraft to demonstrate over Bajil, and two Sopwith Snipe aircraft were accordingly transferred to Kamaran with three RAF officers and eight aircraftmen. The first flight was made on November 24, and two mornings later one aircraft flew over Bajil to reconnoitre the position of the party. No bombs were dropped. This flight has been quoted as the first example of aircraft being used in a peacetime internal security role, and an apparently authoritative publication of the time said that two aircraft secured the release of the mission. This was far from the truth. The appearance of the aircraft certainly had some value but only as a contributory cause. Negotiations for the mission's release were still in progress at Hodeida when one aircraft flew over Bajil narrowly avoiding a forced landing because of engine trouble. Being market day, Bajil was full of armed tribesmen who fired indiscriminately at the aircraft, and after it had flown off they opened fire on the house where the mission was staying, keeping up the fusillade for fifteen minutes. The Quhra had been willing to allow the mission to return to Hodeida durings its second week of captivity, but four months passed before the British Government ordered its return to Aden while negotiations were still proceeding between the

British Political Officer at Hodeida and the Quhra. It was not until December 12 that 200 armed Quhra were able to escort the mission back to Hodeida. Later the Imam pleaded that he had been power-less to prevent the mission's detention or to secure its release, in spite of the presence of his soldiers and of the offers of the ransom money.

(ii) THE CLAYTON MISSION, 1923, AND THE 1928 OPERATIONS

The Imam now ordered his armies to invade the Protectorate with the simple object of expelling the colonial power. In 1923 they took Beidha and, in the following year, the upper part of the Audhali territory. The new Resident in Aden had been instructed to enter into peaceful negotiations with the Imam. Presents, which included horses and a Ford car, were dispatched from Aden to the palace at Sana. The palace reciprocated and appointed as Yemeni representative in Aden Qadi Abdullah al-Arashi, who stayed there about two years trying to conclude a treaty; but the con-tinued presence of the Idrisi in the Yemeni ports contributed largely to his lack of success. Six months after the Imam had written to Ankara in June 1923 asking if he could send a Deputy to the Turkish Grand Assembly (to enlist Turkish political support against the British), Lieutenant-Colonel Jacob again tried to negotiate with the Imam. This time he reached Sana and in December 1923 tried to arrange for a permanent British diplomatic representative in the Yemeni capital; for an extension of the Aden-Lahej railway to Sana, and for the granting of favourable trade concessions. In return the Imam was offered recognition of his sovereignty over the Sultanate of Lahej and over the Hadhramaut. Jacob was received with indifference, and he returned to Hodeida with nothing achieved but the publication of a manifesto by the Imam in which he expressed a desire for friendly relations with Great Britain. Even so, further frontier violations occurred and, on July 9, 1925, two aircraft from Aden were used to try to force the Yemenis to retire from the upper Audhali territory. In the following October, aircraft, this time operating from Shuqra landing strip, were again used in an effort to regain lost ground in Audhali territory. In 1926 the Imam seized part of the lower Audhali territory but was ejected by air operations. These operations prompted the British to take the initiative, and the next year Sir Gilbert Clayton, returning from successful negotiations with the Ibn Saud on the Saudi Arabian frontiers with Trans-jordan and Iraq, was cordially welcomed by the Imam at Sana. Sir Gilbert, whose mission lasted from January 24 to February 21, 1926, aimed at settling the frontier question and negotiating a treaty of friendship. However as the Imam claimed all of south-west Arabia he returned from Sana empty-handed, to discover that Signor Jacopo Gasparini, Governor of Eritrea, had succeeded where he had failed. On September 2, 1926, the ten-year agree-ment, afterwards known as the Italo-Yemeni Treaty of 1926, was published. The Germans had also wooed much of the Imam's enthusiasm away from the British, for in 1926 they also sent Herr Weiss-Sonnenburg, their Ambassador in Addis Ababa, to conclude a treaty of friendship.

In 1927 there was a Yemeni incursion to the Subeihi village of Am Myza, only checked on October 9 when the tribesmen were forced to withdraw after warning notices had been dropped by the Royal Air Force. By now the Imam's countrymen had encroached up to a point only forty miles from Aden. The next year, the responsibility for the defence of the Colony was transferred from the War Office to the Air Ministry (the saving in cost being estimated at £100,000 per year). As long before as October 1926, the Resident, Major-General Sir J. H. Keith-Stewart, had esti-mated that one Indian Division with only one battery of artillery, and the normal Aden garrison would be required to recapture Dhala. He also recommended that the Royal Air Force detachment (the Aden Flight) should be increased to one squadron. Whitehall did not however see fit to act upon the Resident's proposals and it was fortunate that no further serious incursions were made into the Protectorate until the spring of 1928, when the Imam's commander at Qataba captured and imprisoned two sheikhs from the Protectorate. A truce was granted to the Imam on March 25 after some of his frontier towns had been bombed and the two sheikhs were released. On June 5 the Imam asked for an extension of the truce until July 17 but he refused a British request to evacuate Dhala by June 20 as a sign of good faith. Consequently, a demonstration flight of eight aircraft of No. 8 Squadron (Squadron Leader G. H. Bowman, DSO, MC) flew over the principal Yemeni towns as far north as Dhamar. On this flight pamphlets were dropped, warning the Yemenis that if Dhala were not

C*

evacuated by June 24 they would possibly be bombed, but in spite of the influence of the Imam's commander at Taizz and of Seif al-Islam Muhamad, the Imam's eldest son, who were both opposed to hostilities, no action was taken by the Imam to evacuate Dhala and reinforcements were sent by him to Qataba and Taizz.

In the face of this provocation, Taizz was heavily bombed on the morning and evening of June 25, and during the following week forty-seven bombing sorties were made against Yemeni garrisons in the Mafalis, Qataba and Dhala areas; some bombs were also dropped on Yerim. The Yusifiyin had turned out the Imam's garrisons from several of their villages in the Mafalis area and Muhamad Noman, the Imam's senior commander of the area, called for reinforcements to prevent a revolt of the Shafai. The Koteibi had captured the Imam's southernmost outpost at As-Sulaiq by June 28 and Qataba, Dhala, Dhamar and the Mavia–Mafalis area were bombed during the second week of air operations. On July 3 the Imam's forces counter-attacked at As-Sulaiq, but the Koteibi, having held them at bay, advanced to Al-Hamra and on July 9 the Imam's garrison was turned out of Urkub by the Bakni of the Radfan group, thus clearing the Radfan area of Yemeni troops. In the meantime the Amir of Dhala, accompanied by Flight-Lieutenant A. R. M. Rickards, AFC, with a pack radio set, moved to As-Sulaiq in order to organise a local tribal force, but the near-mutinous tribesmen refused to advance. Major T. C. Fowle, the acting Resident, and the Sultan of Lahej were then flown to the village to enforce discipline; their efforts were successful and the Amir of Dhala was able to collect a force of about 1,000 men at Al-Hauta by July 14 and to occupy Dhala, where the Amir soon established himself. Some attempt was made by the Imam's troops between August 1 and 5 to recapture the town; but their advance was checked when Awabil and Sana were bombed. As a result of further bombing of Awabil, the village was occupied by Protectorate tribes on August 15. In spite of the general success of these air operations, which had turned his forces out of most of the Dhala Amirate, the Imam still retained control of the Audhali Plateau, continued to threaten the Wadi Beihan and to raid into the Subeihi country. Three months later he signed a treaty of friendship with the Soviet Union. Mr. James Loder Park, American Vice-Consul in Aden, who had been at Sana in August and had discussed the situation with the Imam afterwards, reported that the bombing had had a very great moral effect throughout the Yemen. Trade had been brought to a standstill and two-thirds of the inhabitants of Sana were driven to living in the surrounding countryside. Tribesmen had blamed the Imam for having failed to make peace, and there was a general feeling that it was useless to fight against aircraft.

Once more the Imam turned to Turkey. This time he sent Ahmad Effendi, one of the former Turkish officers in his service, to Ankara with a leter to Mustapha Kemal. The only outcome of this overture was that Ahmad Effendi stayed in Ankara as the Yemeni representative in Turkey.

Constant frontier clashes occurred during the next few years, particularly in the Dhala and Beihan areas. In March 1930, for instance, reports were received in Aden that the Yemenis were concentrating troops at Rada with the object of attacking Beihan but the sight of three reconnaissance aircraft caused the Yemenis to disperse. Nevertheless, two months later, the Zeidi news-sheet *Al-Imam* reported that the people of Al-Juaba in the Murad district had made representations about the insecurity of their country and that Sherif Abdullah al-Domain had been sent by the Imam to restore order and establish an administration. This report was received in Aden with some suspicion, particularly as the government's information was that Al-Domain had occupied Al-Juaba on May 1 with a force of approximately 3,000 men, three guns and a large supply column. The Beihan tribes believed that it was the Imam's intention to occupy their territory. Consequently, Lieutenant-Colonel Maurice Lake (who in 1919 had raised the 1st Yemeni Infantry in Aden) and a Beihan tribesman were taken on air reconnaissances on May 26, 27 and 30, so that they could annotate photographs which could be used in any future operations.

(iii) FRONTIER INCIDENTS 1931-4

The Imam persisted in initiating propaganda and martial demonstrations in the south. In 1931 he occupied the villages of Al-Ain belonging to the Masabi, who were allied to the Sherif of Beihan. The frontier in this area had not been demarcated, but as the result of a reconnaissance in March 1931 it was concluded that the Al-Ain area was within the Beihan sphere both geographically and politically. An ultimatum instructing the Imam to evacuate all the Masabi territory with a threat of air action was sent to him on September 25 and, on October 5, air reconnaissances were carried out over Rada, Jaufa and other areas in the Yemen, and notices were being dropped to warn the inhabitants of the possibility of air action being taken. The Yemeni forces evacuated Al-Ain on October 4 but took care to loot and burn a number of villages as they withdrew. The Aden Government were still considering what compensation to claim for the damage done, when new treaty proposals were received from the Imam. As these proposals represented a considerable advance on any previously received, the matter was allowed to drop.

The Royal Air Force was not always used as a weapon against the Yemen, and its aeroplanes at Aden often assisted the Protectorate tribes and individuals in the Yemen. On May 8, 1932, for instance, an urgent radio message was received in Aden via Kamaran from Seif al-Islam Ahmad, asking for a British doctor to be sent to him at Hodeida. Wing Commander B. A. Playne, the RAF Principal Medical Officer, and Flight Lieutenant A. H. Montgomery, flew to Kamaran the next day and then via Ibn Abbas to Hodeida. Wing Commander Playne advised the Prince of the course of treatment which he should follow and after his return to Aden on May 11 sent a full medical report for the Prince to see. Seif al-Islam Ahmad's health improved and he travelled to Hajja on May 24. The Resident received warm messages of thanks from the Prince and the Imam, and the Prince was reported to have expressed an earnest desire that the differences between Aden and the Yemen would soon be settled.

In spite of these friendly overtures and the creation of temporary goodwill, further attacks were made on the Protectorate. In June 1933 Yemeni tribesmen and soldiers attacked the village of Am-Nabia, in the Subeihi country, and later penetrated to the coast; but an ultimatum from Aden resulted in the Imam withdrawing all his forces. The Imam had by now realised that sooner or later he would have to choose between peace and war with Aden. In addition, the tension on his northern frontier had already developed into skirmishes with Saudi troops. Representatives of Ibn Saud and Imam Yahya had met at Maidi in March 1933 in an attempt to reach an agreement on their frontier, but the talks were unsuccessful; later, when Ibn Saud sent representatives to Sana, the

Imam kept them as hostages and proceeded to overrun Najran and Asir. In April 1934 the sporadic fighting gave way to full-scale hostilities, and Jizan, Maidi and Hodeida were soon in the hands of Ibn Saud. During the next month HMS *Penzance* (Commander R. H. Bevan) reported to Aden that Yemeni troops had evacuated Hodeida, that law and order had ceased to exist in the town and the lives and property of some 300 Indian inhabitants were in danger. At the request of Commander Bevan a demonstration flight was made over the town by some aircraft of No. 8 Squadron, which afterwards remained at Kamaran for a few days until Hodeida was occupied by Saudi forces and order was restored. Italy and France were also concerned at the possible danger to their subjects at Hodeida during this period and HMS *Penzance* was joined in the Hodeida roadstead by three armed Italian vessels from Massawa and an old French submarine chaser.

(iv) THE TREATY OF SANA 1934

In the meantime, in 1932, control of Aden had passed to the Governor-General at Delhi, and the Resident at Aden had become Chief Commissioner. Colonel Bernard Reilly, in post as Resident at that time, and a member of Jacob's mission in 1919, became first Chief Commissioner, in later years coming to be regarded as the father of Aden Colony. Colonel Reilly had been waiting for a suitable occasion to find the Imam off his guard and, after the withdrawal of the Yemeni troops from the Subeihi country as a result of the June 1933 ultimatum, he saw that the time was opportune – particularly as he foresaw that it was only a question of time before the Imam would be at war with Ibn Saud in the north. The Imam well knew that in dealing with Colonel Reilly he would be assured of a facesaving, if rigorous, capitulation. The time had therefore come to start negotiations in earnest for an Anglo-Yemeni treaty. Making the first move, on December 2, the Political Secretary, Mr. (later Sir) Reginald Champion, was flown to Lodar to warn the Audhali Sultan to maintain peace with his rival on the Dhahir Plateau above Lodar, in anticipation of its evacuation by the Imam. Withdrawal from the upper Audhali country and from the remaining posts in the Dhala Amirate was a prerequisite for the signature of the treaty, imposed upon the Imam by Colonel Reilly. On December 15, Reilly and Captain

R. A. B. Hamilton (later Lord Belhaven) left Aden in HMS *Hastings* (Captain C. S. Sandford, OBE) on their way to Sana: Champion, who had been delayed by sickness, was flown to Kamaran on December 22 to join them. After long and protracted negotiations carried out between Colonel Reilly, Mr. Champion and Ragheb Bey, the Yemeni 'Foreign Minister,' the treaty was eventually signed on February 11, 1934. Among other matters the Imam recognised a *status quo* frontier similar to that agreed with the Turks some thirty years before. Significantly, no mention was made of the Anglo-Turkish Boundary Commission of 1902–5 in the text of the treaty and, for the first time, Great Britain recognised Imam Yahya as King of the Yemen – a palliative if nothing else. Sir Gilbert Clayton's negotiations in Sana in 1926 had broken down because of the Imam's adherence to his claim to the whole of South-west Arabia including Aden and the Protectorates. This claim was based upon the fact that Zeidi Imams had ruled the whole area from about 1630 up to the time of the secession of the Sultan of Lahej in 1728. In 1933 the Imam still upheld this claim, while the British maintained their claim to all territory up to the Anglo-Turkish line of 1905. At the time of the signature of the Treaty of Sana in 1934, all the Imam's forces had been forced to withdraw behind this line with the exception of those still occupying the Sultanate of Beidha. This then was the *status quo* frontier which the Treaty of Sana accepted. Under its provisions Great Britain did not assert its claim to Beidha, and the Imam did not repeat his to Aden and the Protectorates. The treaty in fact purposely did not involve the renunciation of territorial claims by either Great Britain or the Yemen but was designed to ensure that the frontier remained, for forty years, as it was at the time of the signature.

Captain Basil Seager, an official in the British Legation at Jedda on secondment for three months to Aden, was flown to Lodar on January 17, while the treaty negotiations were in progress, to supervise the taking over of the Dhahir Plateau. Having been transferred to the Colonial Administrative Service in 1934, Seager spent some time in that year at Bir Uzia with an official appointed by the Imam, attempting to resolve disagreements on boundary questions. He returned to Aden on December 7, and shortly afterwards fighting again broke out on the Subeihi border at a point where the final boundary line had still to be settled.

Messages were dropped by the Royal Air Force on December 24 at Al-Ghurig and at Al-Shab warning the villagers to stop fighting, and asking them to wait for the publication of a friendly settlement which was being arranged. As as outcome of the Treaty of Sana Captain Seager had been appointed the British frontier officer (a Yemeni frontier officer was also appointed) and was to make many such visits to the Yemen in future years. On a visit in 1936 he had to obtain the Imam's permission to motor twenty miles from Sana for a picnic. The journey, which was made under close surveillance, was cut short when it was discovered that he was travelling in the direction of Marib, always an area forbidden to foreign travellers. While in Sana in 1937, he attempted to obtain permission for the Royal Air Force to lay out certain landing grounds in the Yemen, but his request was met with a blunt refusal, the result of Italian intervention. In February 1938, on a similar visit, he tried to bring about a settlement of the frontier question, once again without success.

(v) IMPROVED ANGLO-YEMENI RELATIONS

The Treaty of Sana brought peace to the Aden–Yemen frontier. Although occasional problems arose and skirmishes occurred at the border between Protectorate and Yemeni tribes, relations between Great Britain and Imam Yahya continued to be reasonably cordial. But the question of the international status of the Shabwa region caused some trouble in 1938: in the late autumn, Al-Gardai, an ex-Governor of the Harib province of the Yemen, occupied Shabwa proclaiming it to be within the Imam's territory. An ultimatum from Aden was presented to the Imam at Sana by Captain Seager on November 17; however it was disregarded, and Captain R. A. B. Hamilton at the head of a force of Government Guards and about 250 tribesmen forced Al-Gardai's surrender. The ex-Governor's men were escorted to the frontier, Al-Gardai himself being flown as far as Nuqub on his way to Marib. Because reprisals were expected Captain Hamilton remained at Shabwa for some weeks, but it was not until June 1939 that the Imam protested to Great Britain against the occupation of what he claimed to be his own territory. Great Britain replied in friendly vein promising an amicable settlement, and when Seif al-Islam Ahmad visited London in 1939 he was assured of British friendship.

The improvement in Anglo-Yemeni relations brought about by the Treaty of Sana enabled the Aden authorities to turn their attention to the pacification of the Protectorate, and between 1937 and 1954 no less than thirteen states in the Protectorate agreed to 'accept the advice' of the Governor of Aden in all matters connected with the welfare and development of their territory. Small forces of locally recruited Tribal Guards were formed in many states to assist the ruler in maintaining order and internal security. In addition, a force of Government Guards under British and Arab officers was organised to supplement the Tribal Guards. Both these native forces acted in a civil police role. Although, between 1934 and 1939, most of the British effort in Aden was directed toward the Protectorate, Great Britain found it necessary also to keep a watchful eye on the gradual development of foreign infiltration into the Yemen. The Italians had always been the most prominent and the most successful in this field.

(vi) THE THREAT FROM ITALY 1861–1943

On their expedition to Abyssinia in the 1830's the brothers d'Abbadie took with them a young Lazzarist named Guiseppe Sapeto. Over the years Sapeto persistently urged his government to stake some claim in the Red Sea in order to use the great opportunities it offered for trade and fishing. After the Italian union of 1861, Italy – whose eastern Mediterranean trade was now practically non-existent and whose route to the East would become the shortest among the principal European powers, once the Suez Canal was opened – was ready for limited colonial expansion. After an abortive attempt to establish a penal colony in the Red Sea in 1867, she purchased for the Rubatino Shipping Company the bay of Assab on the Eritrean coast in 1869. Assab was occupied by Italian troops in 1885, and Massawa was taken at the same time. It was natural at this time that Italy should look to the Yemen for friendly relations. Renzo Manzoni, a son of the novelist, had already toured the Yemen extensively before 1880, and Moshe Schapira, an Italian-Jewish dealer in antiquities from Jerusalem, spent four months in the country in 1878 when he travelled from Hodeida to Sana and returned through Dhamar to the coast at Aden. Luigi and Guiseppe Caprotti were sent to Sana in 1883 to represent the Italian general trading firm of Mazzucchelli e Perera, in theory as export-import salesmen, but in fact planted to supply intelligence to Rome on Yemeni and British political and military activity.Luigi died on January 10, 1889, but his brother remained in the town until 1918 when, as an old man, he was forced to return home. In 1871 the Italians asked the British Government for permission to buy Socotra; although they were refused, they made secret attempts to occupy it during the following few years. Manzoni's book on the Yemen was well known when another appeared from the hand of Gian Battista Rossi, who spent three months in Sana during the Imam's revolt against the Turks in 1891. Ferdinando Martini, one of the pioneer explorers of Eritrea, and appointed Governor in 1898, proved himself during his nine years in office superior to most of his successors. He was able to spread a favourable impression of his country by enlisting Yemenis into his military and labour corps and sending them back to their homeland with money and a good word for the Italians. The Marchese Gaetano Benzoni was sent to Mocha in December 1909 on a further recruiting mission, and joined the German explorer Hermann Burkhardt on a journey to the interior, but both he and Burkhardt were assassinated in mysterious circumstances and the murderers were never discovered. Early in the twentieth century the Italians showed an interest in constructing a railway from Hodeida to Sana, but the contract was awarded to a French syndicate. During the Italo-Turkish War, the newly built railway installations near Hodeida suffered slightly from bombardment by the Italian Navy, which blockaded the Yemeni Red Sea ports and also bombarded Mocha and Sheikh Said. After the end of the war in October 1912 a medical aid hostel was established by the Italians at Hodeida and by 1920 the wireless station and the harbour works at the port were both operated by Italians. In 1919, at the Versailles peace conference, the Italian Government received little favour, but by 1925 the situation was very different, the Fascist régime having becoming firmly entrenched, and with Mussolini well on the way to raising his country's status to that of a major power. Being by then well established in Eritrea, Italy again turned her eyes to the opposite shores of the Red Sea with the thought of gaining increased security for her East African colonies and seeking additional economic advantage. Dr. Jacopo Gasparini, the first Fascist Governor of Eritrea, was given the task of establishing the first formal contact with the Imam. Having by now consolidated her position in the eastern Mediterranean by the colonisation of Libya, Italy was preparing to outflank Aden and create for herself a South Arabian empire. To this end, friendship with the Yemen would give Italy easy access to Aden, besides good port facilities.

Gasparini signed a treaty of friendship with the Imam at Sana on September 2, 1926. The treaty was to last for ten years; it was the first European treaty to acknowledge Imam Yahya as King of the Yemen and it included arrangements for certain commercial concessions. An Italian Air Force officer, Captain Arrigoni, who was a member of the treaty mission, had the distinction of landing the first aeroplane, a Sva, at Sana and presenting it to the Imam. Among the distinguished members of the mission was Massimo Rava, who in the following year published a comprehensive work on Eritrea. After the treaty was signed, more Italian aeroplanes were sent to Sana and, taking a keen interest in them, the Imam had several Yemenis trained as pilots in Egypt, and established a primitive flying school at Sana. As it turned out the Imam's enthusiasm was soon curbed because, for many years afterwards, he felt constrained to forbid flying – the reason being that a member of the royal household had died in an aircraft accident when two aircraft flown by Germans collided over Sana. After this the few remaining Italian aeroplanes were left to rot in their hangars. This did not however deter Italy from forming the Italo-Arabian Company which, very soon after the conclusion of the 1926 treaty, proceeded to work up a considerable trade in the export of petroleum products to the Yemen.

On June 1, 1927, less than a year after the first Italian treaty was signed, a secret agreement was concluded between Italy and the Yemen. It dealt mainly with the supply of Italian armaments to the Imam and, after the secret leaked out, it gave rise to some international condemnation not only because of the armaments question but because Italian commercial enterprise was, under the secret agreement, to be given preferential treatment in the Yemen. The 'leak' of information about this second treaty may well have been engineered at the time of the visit of the Imam's eldest son, Seif al-Islam Muhamad, and Ragheb Bey the Yemeni Foreign Minister to Naples and Rome in July 1927. Perhaps because it did not wish to appear upset by these supposedly startling revelations, the British Government felt obliged to make some face-saving and nonchalant announcement on the subject. In August 1927, a statement was made in the House of Commons that Great Britain did not really resent Italy's preferential position in the Yemen trade and that her interests would not be harmed by the Italo-Yemeni treaties; neither would any British negotiations with the Imam be adversely affected. (Despite these parliamentary assurances, there was consternation in the British press where there was no doubt that the Imam had been forced into allowing the Italians a trading monpoly in the Yemen.) Nevertheless it was quite true that the trade in skins was being diverted from Aden to Massawa, and Italian assistance in the form of aeroplanes and munitions had been given to the Imam so that he could protect himself against the still threatening attitude of Ibn Saud at his northern frontier. However, although earnestly wanting support against both Ibn Saud and the British, the Imam was careful never to deliver himself wholly into Italian hands. Sir Stewart Symes took over the Residency in Aden from Major General Keith-Stewart in 1928, and the Italian Government took some local measures to placate the British temper of the time. Signor Zoli, Governor of Eritrea, invited Symes informally to stay with him in Asmara. Permission was sought and obtained from the Foreign Office, and Symes took advantage of the visit to persuade Zoli to curb Italian intrigue in the Yemen. Ingeniously, he told Zoli that the Italian Government considered the forward policy, which Gasparini (Zoli's predecessor) had pursued in the Yemen, to be too costly and that he might care to consider a less aggressive approach in the future. However, in spite of the personal friendship which grew up between the two governors, in its diplomatic aspect the visit was not very successful.

During the years following the 1926 and 1927 treaties the Imam's wish to have the services of European doctors was used by the Italians as a means of maintaining agents in the country. Dr. Merucci, for instance, first went to the Yemen in 1936 and remained there for more than twenty years. Cesare Ansaldi was for many years the Imam's personal physician and was able to travel extensively, practising among many Yemeni tribes from 1929 onwards. But in 1934, Ibn Saud defeated the Imam who was trying by means of frontier operations to expand into Saudi

Arabia. Ibn Saud's numbers were superior and the Yemenis were ill-organised. Italian intentions thereby suffered a considerable setback; the Treaty of Sana in that year was a moral victory for the British and, at the time of the negotiations for the Treaty of Taif in May 1934 between Saudi Arabia and the Yemen, Ibn Saud had insisted that Italian infiltration into the Yemen should be discouraged. But in 1936 the Italo-Yemeni Treaty of 1926 was renewed for a further year; the Italian agent-doctors remained and one of them, Ettore Rossi, toured the country that year. The Imam had never up to this time succeeded in producing his own small arms ammunition without European help and, from 1920 onwards, he relied upon an Austrian, George Ghericich, to run his cartridge factory in Sana. The factory, located in the Qasr Ghamdan, the citadel of Sana, which also housed the gaol and the mint, refilled old cartridge cases and cast primitive bullets for them. The lead was imported and the nitrate produced locally. By 1925 a munitions factory to replace the one operated by Ghericich was instituted and an Italian, Romolo Cipressi, an ex-employee of *Bologna Pirotecnica*, was placed in charge. Cipressi undertook what might be called the first technical development in the Yemen; and having taken on the project, he set out to provide the necessary equipment. He arrived at Hodeida on February 26, 1926, with much of the machinery required but it was not until over a year later that all the necessary supplies and equipment eventually arrived at Sana. After much more delay the first cartridges were produced in the early months of 1928, Subsequently Cipressi became, in a sense, chief engineer to the Imam, entrusted with all public engineering projects. He installed a water pumping plant at Rhauda after the cartridge factory was in production, and he surveyed a route for a road between Hodeida and Sana. Italy finally claimed him back in the 1930s and he rose to a responsible position in the *Bologna Pirotecnica*, his work in the Yemen being continued by an oddly assorted quartet of Italian technicians – a general mechanic, a founder, a wireless operator and a cabinet maker.

Italian interest in the Yemen reached a high level in the mid-1930s. Salvator Aponte's book on the Yemen appeared in Rome in 1936 and in the following year Gasparini again led a full diplomatic mission, accompanied by much pomp and circumstance, to the Imam at Sana. Italian Government funds were lavishly dispensed on this occasion, and a new treaty of friendship was signed. Among its provisions was the *de jure* recognition by the Imam of Italian sovereignty in Abyssinia. At this time, the Imam's personal physician had for many years been Dr. Emilio Dubiossi, who was assisted by nearly a dozen other Italian doctors. In 1938 Mussolini had seven 'diplomatic' representatives in the Yemen, while Great Britain's sole agent was a political clerk, Salah Ja'afar, whose existence was merely tolerated by the Imam and whose activities were confined to the area of Hodeida.

However some attempt was made early in 1938 by the Italians to come to terms with the British. In April the Anglo-Italian Agreement was signed, the terms of which in effect put an end to Italian dreams of creating a South Arabian empire. Italy and Great Britain agreed to respect the independence and integrity of the Yemen, and not to seek special advantage in either the Yemen or Saudi Arabia. Italian influence predominated in the Yemen well into the war of 1939–45, two pro-Axis broadcasting stations continuing to operate there until they were finally closed down by the Imam. Although in the early days of the war the Imam continued his anti-British propaganda, mainly through the medium of his newssheet *Al-Imam*, the rout of the Germans at El-Alamein caused him to modify his tirade against the Allied cause and on February 26, 1943, he finally severed relations with the Axis powers. The members of the Italian medical mission were interned or expelled under pressure from the British authorities in Aden.

(vii) FRANCE AND THE RAILWAY PROJECT 1909–12

While the Italian activity in the Yemen was more intensive than that of any other European country between 1918 and 1939, there was no lack of French interest in the country. Early in the century she had made a bold attempt to gain a foothold in the economy of the Yemen, and so supplement her efforts on the opposite shores of the Red Sea. Between 1902 and 1908 a jetty and some breakwaters were being slowly constructed at Hodeida: the contract for these works had been awarded to a French engineer who, in his turn, had subcontracted them to an Italian. However, the whole project was so inadequately supervised by the Ottoman Government that only when the 'harbour' was completed was it discovered how hopelessly unsatisfactory it was –

a folly which had cost the Ottoman Government some £14,000 Sterling. Until the early 1950s, when it was cleared, this small boat harbour, formed by two moles and a breakwater was so silted up that loaded lighters could not use the quays, and only dhows of the smallest draft could enter. Ocean-going dhows and steamships still had to anchor in the roads two or three miles offshore.

After 1906 the Turks made plans for the construction of a deep water harbour of five fathoms at Jebhane Inlet, seventeen kilometres north of Hodeida, between Ras Khatib and the mainland. It was intended that anchorage should be provided for twelve ships which could discharge simultaneously at a stone quay, and this harbour at Ras Khatib was to be linked by railway to Hodeida. The contract and concession for railway and port constructions were awarded to a French syndicate headed by the Banque Française pour le Commerce et de l'Industrie and called the Ottoman Hodeida–Sana and Branch Line Railway Company The contract was worth about £2,000,000. In February 1909 A. Zaborowski, consulting engineer to the syndicate, proposed that A. J. Beneyton, a Frenchman who had worked under him in Turkey and China, should direct the surveys. Beneyton's first mission to the Yemen lasted from August 1909 to July 1910. The result was a project for a railway to run from Ras Khatib through Hodeida, Bajil, Obal and Sana to Amran via the Wadi Siham and Wadi Ferch. This proposal was not accepted in its entirety owing to financial considerations and to the insecurity of the surrounding country, but a line across the Tihama through Bajil to Hajile was sanctioned and work was begun. Beneyton undertook a further journey between January 1911 and November 1912 to decide upon an alternative route which would run through some of the richest centres of the territory – Beit al-Faqih, Zabid, Taizz, Ibb, Yerim, Dhamar, Maber, Sana and Amran, but the Ottoman Government approved expenditure on the line only as far as Taizz. In the meantime engineers had arrived from Europe to start work at Ras Khatib, and in March 1911 railway construction started without there being in existence any proper arrangements for the landing of the heavy material. After nine months, equipment worth two million francs lying at Ras Khatib had become useless, and by the end of 1911 nearly £500,000 had been spent, no harbour had been made and Ras Khatib had not been joined by railway with Hodeida; only five miles of metre-gauge track were ever laid. The project was quickly abandoned after the Italians bombarded Hodeida during the Italo-Turkish War of 1912. In 1913 the stout corrugated iron buildings at Ras Khatib were still in good condition, but a locomotive with two passenger coaches was left derelict on the line and the temporary jetty, built at Ras Khatib to land stone brought from Zoukar Island, was still in existence. The grandiose project had come to nothing. This pitiful example of Ottoman inefficiency being too much for the French to bear, they abandoned any further enterprise in the Yemen for the time being, although in August 1912 they appointed their first Vice-Consul to Hodeida, M. Roux. During 1914-18, most of the 1,400-strong Somali battalion of the French Army was recruited in the Yemen. Four hundred were killed during the war and the battalion received a special army citation for its bravery.

The French were very active in the Yemen during the decade beginning in 1922. An oil prospector, Vincent Cherruau, landed at Mocha in that year and travelled through Taizz to Sana. He was followed soon afterwards by M. Sicard who was so well received by the Imam that he stayed in Sana for several weeks while negotiations were in progress for the Imam's purchase of a wireless station which would enable him to communicate directly with Djibouti. Cherruau was again in the Yemen in 1929 and landing at Hodeida he managed, after visiting Sana, to reach Hajja and Amran and to travel some distance along the Wadi Bana.

There had been many attempts by European nations to extract oil from the Red Sea islands both before and after the 1914-18 war. Not to be left out of the race, the French decided that the Yemen should be the area for their oil prospecting. Consequently in 1931 General Gassouin, Director of the Franco-American Standard Oil Company, decided to send a mission composed of two American oil geologists, Fred Ely and R. A. MacGovern, to find out whether oil drilling would be profitable. Pierre Lamare, a geologist, was selected by a French corporation to search for metal deposits in the country. Lamare was also commissioned by the Natural History Museum of Paris to undertake a geological survey, and joining Ely and MacGovern at Djibouti he left for Mocha, also accompanied by Cherruau, who had been appointed organiser of the expedition. From Mocha the party went to Sana via Taizz,

Yerim, Ibb and Dhamar and left by the Dhamar–Yerim–Qataba–
Dhala route for Aden. Expensive gifts were presented to the
Imam and the French offered to open up Mocha as a port, buy
coffee in large quantities and sell arms and ammunitions to the
Yemen Government; but they came away without any positive
assurances from the Imam.

Another attempt to win the favour of the Iman was made in 1932
when a French survey ship discovered the makings of a good
harbour about half a mile to the north of Hodeida, but the
approach miscarried after the Imam had refused their offer to
develop a port there free of charge. A similar reverse had been
experienced two years previously after the failure of the Maigret
Mission. Roger Maigret, the French Minister at Jedda and a
veteran of the military and political administration in Morocco,
led a delegation to the Imam in 1930 in an attempt to conclude a
treaty of friendship. The mission failed because it would not agree
to the Imam's request for the recognition of his sovereignty over
the western part of the Aden protectorate and the Hadharmaut.
It was not until six years later that some success was achieved.
In 1936 Professor Robert Montagne, director of the Institut
Musulman de Damas and founder and director of the Centre
des Hautes Etudes d'Administration Musulmane de Paris, spent
several weeks in the Yemen, and on April 25 a Treaty of Friendship
was signed at Sana by Roger Maigret and Ragheb Bey, the Foreign
Minister. But there were still problems to be solved, and difficulties
arose because the French would not renounce their claim to
Sheikh Said, which they asserted was still under concession to
them from 1870. However, the treaty was finally ratified at Sana
nearly a year later, on February 4, 1937, and published in the
Journal Officiel in Paris on April 22. These easier official relations
with the Imam enabled the eminent archaeologist Dr. Jules
Barthoux and his photographer Clément to visit some ruins in
the Wadi Kharid area in 1938, but it was not until the next year
that further diplomatic approaches were made. To try and allay
the Imam's discontent on the subject of Sheikh Said, the French
Minister at Jedda at that time, M. Ballereau, sent him a declaration
saying that France would not insist on her rights to Sheikh Said
if the Imam would agree not to grant concessions in his country
to any other nation. War interrupted the negotiations and it was
not until 1946 that France and the Yemen finally came to terms.

(viii) AMERICANS, GERMANS, DUTCH AND JAPANESE, 1920–40

Only about twenty Americans travelled into the Yemen before 1945. Dr. Samuel Zwemer of the Arabian Mission of the Dutch Reformed Church of America visited Sana in 1892 and 1894; another missionary Charles F. Camp, and his wife went up to Sana from Hodeida in 1905 and spent some years in the area, finally settling at Manakha. Later, it seems, Camp was murdered by the Turks, and Charles K. Moser, then United States Consul in Aden, had to journey there five years afterwards to inquire into his death. Amin Rihani, an American-Syrian, made a long journey through the Yemen in 1921 and 1922, ostensibly in the cause of Pan-Arabism. The oil prospecting during that period by Fred Ely and R. A. MacGovern proved fruitless. Charles Crane, an American businessman and philanthropist with a life-long interest in the Arab world, went to see the Imam at Sana at the beginning of 1926, with the object of donating facilities which would help him in developing the country. As a result of this trip Karl Twitchell, an engineer, who has long since become an authority on Saudi Arabia, and Lowe Whiting visited the territory in 1927, and subsequently in 1932 and 1947. These visits, and those of the oil men Fred Ely and R. A. MacGovern in 1923, were not very profitable and certainly no oil was found in commercial quantity, but Twitchell was able to advise on road and bridge making, and the results of these labours can still be seen. In 1925 and 1928 the American Vice-Consul in Aden, James Loder Park, paid goodwill visits to the Imam, and in 1933 Dr. Carleton S. Coon, his wife, and Ralph Forbes, made a short anthropoligical expedition into the country. Two more American oil geologists landed at Hodeida in 1937 to prospect but, like all their predecessors, they had a wasted journey.

As early as 1910 the Farsan Islands were known to contain oil-bearing rocks. Experimental borings were made by a German to whom the Turkish Government had granted a concession, but apart from preliminary work, which failed to produce satisfactory results, no further progress was made before the islands were seized by the Idrisi in 1912. The Germans had already made use of the Farsan Islands some years previously. Sultan Abd el-Hamid had allowed them to establish a coaling station there at the end of 1901; they began by using Khum Island, but transferred their activities in 1902 to the smaller of the two main islands which gave the group its name. The station did not flourish, and was soon abandoned. In March 1913 the German Government tried to arrange with Turkey for the establishment of a coaling station at Mocha. The mission to the Imam in 1926 under Weiss-Sonnenberg, German minister in Addis Ababa, and another delegation to Sana in 1930, which lasted six weeks, were both of little account. The second failed because, like the French, the Germans would not recognise the Imam's sovereignty over the Aden protectorates (more to discomfit the Italians than to please the British). The only success which the Germans ever attained in the Yemen before the end of the Second World War was in their gun running activities in 1934 and 1937; and these were only of a semi-official character.

The Imam concluded treaties of friendship with Abyssinia and Turkey in the 1930s, and in 1932 reached an agreement with Iraq. He signed the Treaty of Taif with Saudi Arabia in May 1934 to end his war with Ibn Saud, and in the spring of 1937 was persuaded to adhere to the Arab Pact of 1936 between Saudi Arabia and Iraq. His signature of the Pact was hailed by the three countries as a great step towards Arab federation, which would serve as a counter to Zionism; however, it was of greater importance as laying some tentative foundation for the formation of the Arab League some nine years afterwards.

Japan did considerable trade in the Yemen between 1933 and 1939, managing to corner 85 per cent of the textile market, the balance being shared between Great Britain, the USA and Italy. Indeed most cotton and all woollen and silk merchandise which was imported into the Yemen before 1939 came from Japan. In 1938 the Imam sent his fourth son, Seif al-Islam Husein, to Tokyo to attend, on May 12, the opening of the first mosque to be built in Japan. Husein, accompanied by a number of Italian 'advisers', sailed in the *Conte Verde* from Brindisi, and a Nippo-Yemenite Association was formed in Tokyo to cement the bonds of friendship between the two countries. After this announcement nothing more was heard of it, and it doubtless fell by the wayside while Japan was preparing for the Second World War.

The five principal foreign contestants for the Imam's favours between 1920 and 1939 were Italy, France, Germany, Japan and Russia. Russia had penetrated the country before 1938, but her activities there only assumed importance from 1950 onwards. Otherwise the Low Countries were the only European nations to enter into any formal relationship with the Imam. A certain Depui, a reserve colonel of the Belgian Army, was for many years the honorary Belgian Consul at Jedda. He had lived in Arab countries for more than thirty years and played the part of a secret agent, putting about stories of his Arab ancestry and assuming the name of Sheikh Ibrahim; in fact he was, amongst other things, a representative of the Fabrique Nationale of Liège and spent much of his time gun-running in the Middle East. He succeeded in gaining the favour of many Arab rulers and when he was in Sana in 1936 a treaty of friendship was concluded between Belgium and the Yemen.

Since the time when their factory at Mocha had fallen into disuse in the eighteenth century the Dutch had had little contact with the Yemen. In 1926, however, a Dutch consulate was established at Jedda so that the interests of Indonesian pilgrims to Mecca could be watched. Dr. Daniel van der Meulen, the famous Dutch explorer of the Hadhramaut, was appointed as Consul, and made a reconnaissance of the Yemen in 1931, travelling from Hodeida to Sana by the southern route. He had a friendly interview with Imam Yahya and visited both Seif al-Islam Ahmad at Hajja, and Seif al-Islam Muhamad who was at that time governor of Hodeida. By 1933 Mr. Adriaanse had become Dutch Consul at Jedda, and in March and April of that year he went to Sana and concluded a treaty of commerce with the Imam. Nine years later van der Meulen, who in the meantime had been reappointed to Jedda, was authorised to pay another courtesy visit to the Imam. The war had made sea transport very scarce and van der Meulen took the overland route from Jedda via Loheia to Hodeida. With the help of Saudi guides he was able to follow the tracks which were made by the Amir Feisal's invading army in the spring of 1934 and he arrived at Sana in August 1942; he returned to the Yemen in 1958 to visit Imam Ahmad at Taizz.

Although there had been a multitude of foreign influences in the Yemen between the two world wars, Great Britain's problems in Aden had been mainly concerned with a settlement of frontier disputes with the Imam Yahya, the neutralisation of Italian influence in the Yemen and the pacification of the hinterland between the coast of the Protectorates and the Yemen. With the onset of the Second World War much of the political effort in Aden was directed towards the question of the Yemen's neutrality.

(ix) THE SECOND WORLD WAR AND ITS PRELIMINARIES

In January 1937, long before the Yemeni tribesmen under Al-Gardai had been forced to evacute Shabwa in November 1938, the Ahl Bal Obeid tribes, whose principal sphere of activity was the Shabwa area, had made friendly overtures to the authorities in Aden. A year later Seif al-Islam Husein was invited to England and on January 3, 1938, he made some friendly comments in a broadcast at the time of the inauguration of the BBC's Arabic Service. But the Imam's displeasure at British contact with the Shabwa tribes was aggravated by the granting of an oil prospecting licence for the whole of the Aden Protectorate to the British company, Petroleum Concessions Ltd. The possibility of there being oil in the Shabwa region had been known to the Imam for a long time and he was naturally anxious to ensure that any prizes obtainable from the area should be to the benefit of his own kingdom. Consequently, not being prepared to agree that Shabwa was within the confines of the Aden Protectorate, he appealed unsuccessfully to Italy to help him press his claim, while the British continued to occupy a small police post at Husn al-Abr, about fifty-five miles north of Shabwa.

Anticipating the war of 1939, the French had tried to extract a promise of Yemeni neutrality from Seif al-Islam Ahmad when he passed through Paris on his way to London in 1939. Ahmad was the bearer of a letter from the Imam to King George VI, protesting against British activities in Shabwa but the letter was written in a friendly vein and contained no threat of reprisals. Nevertheless, when the war did break out in September, in spite of Yemeni incursions into the Wadi Markha and Beihan areas, the Foreign Minister, Ragheb Bey, issued a formal declaration of neutrality. All in all, Anglo-Yemeni relations had continued to be friendly, although the Frontier Officer system gradually fell into abeyance.

One of the best British unofficial ambassadors in the way of maintaining goodwill was Dr. P. W. R. Petrie who was sent to the Yemeni capital early in 1937 in charge of the British Medical Mission to Sana. The mission was composed of members of the Church of Scotland Keith-Falconer Medical Mission at Sheikh

Othman. Dr. Petrie had previously been to the Yemen from Aden in December 1931 when, during a fortnight's stay in Taizz, he attended the daughter-in-law of Seif al-Islam Ahmad; that visit, and the seven year sojourn which he and his wife and child later passed in Sana, went a long way towards maintaining good Anglo-Yemeni relations.

The fall of British Somaliland into Italian hands in 1940 had obvious dangers for the British in Aden, and the Imam, in spite of his declared neutrality, could scarcely have prevented an Italian invasion of the coastal plains of the Tihama. The peoples of the Tihama were mostly Sunni Muslims who were ready to welcome any invader to help them overthrow the Shia Zeidi ruling dynasty. Faced with the problem of convincing the Imam that the British were going to win the war, the Governor of Aden, Sir John Hathorn Hall, wrote to the Imam and proposed that some of the Aden officials should visit him at Sana. The reply was swift and favourable and the Political Adviser at Aden, Colonel Lyall, set out for Sana at the beginning of February 1940. During his six-week stay he was very amicably received by the Imam and the trip was entirely successful. Colonel Lyall had taken along with him his friend Miss Freya Stark, who was working for the Aden Government at the time and who was able to penetrate into the more important harems of Sana and Taizz in order, through feminine influence, to counteract Italian propaganda. The success of Colonel Lyall's interviews with the Imam quickly resulted in a further official visit to the Imam. On his return to Aden, permission was sought and obtained for a further visit, this time by Reginald Champion, who became governor of Aden in 1944. Champion's visit to the Imam in 1940 was chiefly concerned with seeking a solution to the disagreement over the Shabwa problem. No solution was found, but at least the Imam was persuaded to remain in a position of neutrality in the European war. It was necessary, however, to keep up the pressure and in the following year Sir John Hathorn Hall sent his Chief Secretary Harold Ingrams to Sana to discuss the general conduct of frontier affairs. Ingrams, travelling with his wife, reached the capital on April 25, 1941, having passed through Taizz, Mocha and Hodeida. The Ingram's visit had some delayed success, for the Imam broke off diplomatic relations with Italy early in the war and, in December 1941, eight months after his talks with Ingrams, he dismissed the

German Minister in the Yemen. Just over a year afterwards he finally broke with the Axis powers (see page 67) and interned most of their subjects who were currently working in the Yemen.

Towards the end of 1943, there was a serious outbreak of typhus in Sana causing a serious blow to the British Medical Mission there. Miss Cowie, one of the nursing sisters of the mission, herself caught typhus and Dr. Petrie decided to bring her and the rest of the mission to the safety of Aden. Attempts to re-establish the mission were never successful.

Frontier incidents continued during the War, and Dar al-Beidha was occupied for a time in 1941 by Yemeni tribes. A more serious infringement of the frontier occurred in 1943–4 in the extreme south-west of the Protectorate. At the end of 1943 a small Yemeni force was positioned at Haid al-Ma on the Protectorate side of the frontier. Negotiations followed but the Imam managed to prolong them for sixteen months whilst he tried to enlist American, Egyptian and Saudi Arabian help. As his quest for help was abortive he eventually withdrew his troops from Haid al-Ma, with ill-concealed bad grace.

5

A CHANGE OF KING

With Seif al-Islam Ahmad as Governor of Taizz, relations between Great Britain and the Yemen deteriorated quickly after the war, and Ahmad openly encouraged subversive activities in the Aden Protectorate. The Yemen joined the Arab League in 1945 and the United Nations in 1947. In February 1948 Seif al-Islam Abdullah paid a visit to London and sounded a note of encouragement when he asked for a settlement of frontier disputes, a British Minister in Sana and the loan of British technical advisers. While he was on this visit, however, trouble was brewing in his own country and for many weeks the Yemen was to be beset by revolt and bloodshed.

During 1947 there had been a growing discontent within the Imam's kingdom and some moves in outside quarters for the 'liberation' of the Yemen by the Arab League. Rumours had been in circulation for many years about the Imam's failing health, and the succession had been a matter of constant speculation in the bazaars of Sana. These conjectures were aggravated by dissension between the Shafei and the Zeidi and by jealousy among Yahya's sons. There had been talk of the revival of the old Principality of Hodeida and of the Yemeni Liberal Party which had been 'underground' in Aden for some years with the active support of Seif al-Islam Ibrahim. There was a good deal of sympathy for the party in Aden and as long as its stated object was limited to the exhortation of the Imam to grant reforms, and provided that its activities were restricted to expressions of opinion, the Aden authorities did not feel it necessary to interfere. The Party was in fact instituted because of the Imam's severely autocratic methods of government and the rivalry among his sons for the succession.

The Imam's severe ill-health also gave rise to rumours and counter-rumours concerning his death. On the one hand he was reported to be suffering from acute paralysis (hemiplegia), and on the other an earlier report of his death had been denied in 1943. On January 15 that year, he was reported dead, and certain

77

ulema and elders in Sana were supposed to have voted Seiyid Abdullah ibn Ahmad al-Wazir as his successor. This action, they said, conformed 'to the sacred charter accepted by the entire nation before his death'. Al-Wazir's association with this announcement was, however, denied in Egypt, if not in other countries. Seiyid Abdullah ibn Ahmad al-Wazir, aged 60 in 1948, a wealthy landowner and coffee merchant, had, some years previously, been Amir of the *liwa* of Tihama (capital Hodeida) and had represented the Imam at the Treaty of Taif negotiations in May 1934. He was a cousin of the 63-year-old Seiyid Ali al-Wazir, Amir of the South *liwa* (capital Taizz). Both had been deposed from their emirates in favour of the Imam's sons. In 1944, when another of the al-Wazir family, Seiyid Abdulqadus, a son-in-law of Imam Yahya, Amir of the central *liwa* (capital Dhamar), died of typhus, his post was abolished and the whole administration of the country was reorganised. There had been two other *liwas* – Sana, and the North *liwa* (capital Sada) – but this reorganisation, which divided the country into only four administrative areas, placed the reins of local government into the hands of Seif al-Islam Ahmad and Seif al-Islam Motahir in one principality, of Seif al-Islam Abdullah in another and of Seif al-Islam Hasan in the third. The fourth principality, Sana, was to be directly administered by the Imam.

The first open criticism by any Yemeni of Imam Yahya's methods of government was made in Aden on May 14, 1944, by the wealthy Al-Mutib bin Dumaj. On June 4 four other well-known Yemenis joined him in Aden: Sheikh Muhamad Ahmad Noman, Seiyid Zaid al-Mukki, Qadhi Muhamad Mahmoud al-Zubayri and Muhamad al-Shami. An Aden newspaper, *Fatat al-Jazirah*, assisted them by drawing attention to the state of affairs in the Yemen. The Yemeni Liberal Party or Free Yemenis (*Al-Ahrar al-Yemeniyun*) grew from these early discontents. Between October 1944 and February 1945 it remained quiet, mainly on account of the discouragment which it had received from the Aden authorities, but during 1945 and the early part of 1946 the Party began to build up an active propaganda campaign against the Imam, and this was at its height when Seif al-Islam Ahmad visited Aden on April 11, 1946, to try to placate the would-be reformers. He announced to the *Fatat al-Jazirah* that the Yemeni Government would enter into diplomatic relations with the Arab world and would ask for foreign missions to exploit the country's mineral

wealth. Education would, he said, be increased in accordance with
the policy of the Arab League. However, the Free Yemenis were
not satisfied with this announcement and demanded that a constitutional assembly of high officials be established, and that the
Imam's family should be excluded from any governmental post.
For six weeks arguments raged between the Free Yemenis and
the representatives of the Imam until finally, with 30,000 riyals
(about £7,000) subscribed by thirty wealthy Yemenis and by
Shafei merchants from other parts of the Muslim world, the Grand
Yemeni Association (*Al-Jamiat al-Yemeniyat al-Kubra*) was
formed. A new newspaper was also established under the title of
Saut al-Yemen (The Voice of Yemen) and from this press flowed
a large number of books and pamphlets calling for a change in the
system of government. The Free Yemenis and the Grand Yemeni
Association amalgamated in 1946 and on November 21, 1946,
Seif al-Islam Ibrahim came to Aden to join the new movement.

In September 1947 a new campaign was started, poets and
writers directing their efforts towards composing an even greater
volume of anti-government propaganda. A month before the
Imam Yahya was actually killed, an attempt was made in Sana to
murder him. In mid-January 1948, the Grand Yemeni Association
detailed a man to make his way into the palace and assassinate the
Imam. The man succeeded in entering the palace but was appre-
hended by a faithful slave of the royal household before he could
make his way into the room where the Imam was resting. The slave,
Amir Amber, captured him but was unable to hold him in arrest so,
escaping the slave's clutches, the would-be assassin fled the palace,
scaling the outer wall. He passed through the Bir al-Azab quarter
of Sana to join his colleagues and, before he was able to tell
his story, his friends had telegraphed to the outside world that
Imam Yahya had died.

The world's press consequently published news of Imam
Yahya's death while he was still alive, isolated in his palace at Sana.
Qadhi Abdullah al-Amri and Seiyid Husein al-Hilali (at that time
Governor of Hodeida) were his only loyal supporters of any
standing. These reports of the Imam's death in January 1948 and
the election of Al-Wazir as Yahya's successor were soon found to
be incorrect but there had been a meeting in Sana of *ulema* and
notables in January which, having decided to reject the rule of
primogeniture in favour of that of the ancient law of succession,

D

had elected al-Wazir as the new Imam. Just before his death, Imam Yahya, knowing that al-Wazir hoped to usurp the throne, had his gold treasure, worth about £10,000,000, hidden in the countryside by some of his slaves, who were afterwards put to death so that the hiding place should remain a secret. Al-Wazir was said to have discovered the hoard and returned it to Sana but a later announcement from Cairo said that 'the Yemen had asked Great Britain for a loan as the late Imam had hidden all the gold reserve'. In spite of these rumours Imam Yahya's treasury remained intact and was later taken over by Seif al-Islam Ahmad.

In February 1948 further reports – this time true ones – were received in Cairo that Imam Yahya was dead. He had in fact been murdered by machine-gun fire from the cover of a closed lorry on February 17 while he was on his way to visit his farms at Hezjez, to the south of Sana. Fifty bullets were later found in his body. At the same time, Qadhi Abdullah al-Amri, the Prime Minister, was killed at Hezjez, together with Abdul Rahman bin al-Hasan (Abdullah al-Amri's grandson) and one other. Meanwhile at Sana, Jamal Jamil, an Iraqi officer in charge of the disposal of the Imam's treasure, was attempting to hold off the mob bent on breaking into the palace and looting it; here Seif al-Islam Husein and Seif al-Islam Mohsin were killed in the fracas which followed, and Seif al-Islam Yahya surrendered, later to be released on the order of two of his father's supporters, Abdullah Amir Sadaqah and Al-Dasimi.

By February 20, al-Wazir had nominated Seiyid Husein al-Kibsi as his Foreign Minister and had telegraphed to all Arab rulers and governments that he had succeeded Yahya as Imam. The Arab League decided not to recognise the succession of Al-Wazir until a committee of six under the Secretary-General of the Arab League, Azzam Pasha, had visited the Yemen to study the situation, so on February 22 two emissaries of the League, Abdul Monheim Mustafa Bey, of the Egyptian Foreign Office, and Dr. Hasan Ismail, the Commercial Counsellor to the Egyptian Legation at Berne, flew from Cairo to Sana for a preliminary investigation. The mission was received by Seiyid Husein al-Kibsi, but the results of its visit were negative.

As soon as Seif al-Islam Ahmad received news by telegraph from Seif al-Islam Qasim of his father's and brothers' deaths, he

immediately left Taizz, where he had been Amir for the previous
ten years, and, establishing his headquarters at the fortress of
Hajja, where he had also been Amir for some years, prepared for
an attack on al-Wazir. He had a considerable convoy to organise
at Taizz for he took with him to Hajja 180 soldiers in addition to
a car carrying 100,000 riyals and a bag of gold. After passing
through Hodeida, where he was narrowly saved from death at the
hands of a mob with the help of one of al-Wazir's officials who had
deserted, he wandered through the country for a short time in the
disguise of a soldier, rallying most of the Hashid and Bakil tribesmen to his support. Arriving at Hajja on February 22, he found
his brothers Seif al-Islam Abbas and Seif al-Islam Motahir already
there to greet him. From Hajja, Seif al-Islam Ahmad proclaimed
himself 'Commander of the Faithful and Imam of the Yemen',
and he was joined there by many of the mountain tribes, who had
been attracted by rumours of a British invasion and who had
refused to recognise al-Wazir as Imam. Many regular troops of the
Yemeni Army also sided with Seif al-Islam Ahmad who for many
years had been their Commander-in-Chief. At the end of February,
Al-Wazir made an attempt to march against Hajja and, although by
the first week in March complete lawlessness prevailed throughout
the kingdom, he pledged himself to rule as a constitutional king.
He assured his countrymen that he would fight for their welfare
as they had 'long suffered serfdom and privations' and 'could no
longer tolerate despotism and terrorism'. But al-Wazir was
hampered by dissension in his own ranks; the Free Yemenis who
had meanwhile gone to Sana from Aden soon began to disagree
with him, and the two most prominent of them, Muhamad
Mahmoud al-Zubayri and Sheikh Muhamad Ahmad Noman,
quarrelled violently with each other. Not discouraged by such
problems, Al-Wazir tried – unsuccessfully – to charter two aircraft
from the Ethiopian Government for the purpose of collecting
volunteers. Minor clashes took place between Seif al-Islam Ahmad's
and al-Wazir's forces, and on March 13 Seif al-Islam Abbas took
Sana, against little opposition, at the head of 20,000 of his brother's
followers. Although al-Wazir had enjoyed considerable popular
support in and around Sana, he was unable to control his followers,
who became out of hand and took to looting the capital on a grand
scale. With Sana seriously threatened, Al-Wazir asked the Aden
authorities for the loan of an aeroplane in which he could flee to

safety, but the Governor was not inclined to assist the leader of a murderous and usurping faction. Two Egyptian aircraft tried to land at Sana on March 13 to evacuate Egyptian citizens, but they could not land in or near the capital because of the fighting, and had to return to Jedda. On March 14 Seif al-Islam Ahmad made a formal entry into Sana and was duly installed as Imam, adopting the name of An Nasir li din Allah, Supporter of God's Faith.

Al-Wazir had previously dispatched a mission to King Ibn Saud under Seiyid Fadhl al-Wartalani and Abdullah ibn al-Wazir to enlist his support, but Ibn Saud had refused them an audience; Al-Wazir had also asked the governments of Syria, Iraq and Great Britain for military demonstrations in support of his new 'government' but, although nothing was forthcoming from these three countries, a Royal Air Force Wellington aircraft flew over the area to find out what was happening, and British destroyers, including HMS *Comet*, happened, by perhaps more than coincidence, to be carrying out manoeuvres in the Red Sea at that time near Hodeida. In the meantime Seif al-Islam Ibrahim (self-styled Seif al-Haqq, Sword of Right, in defiance of his father Imam Yahya), who had sought refuge in Aden in November 1946 as leader of the Free Yemenis, had taken advantage of the disturbances of 1948 to return to his country and join al-Wazir as his Prime Minister, while Muhamad al-Badr, the son of Seif al-Islam Ahmad, the present Imam, publicly declared himself in opposition to his father. With Sana captured and himself firmly installed, the new Imam Ahmad proceeded to dispose of al-Wazir, sending him, together with his chief henchmen, in captivity to Hajja on April 8, where after summary trial he and thirty of his confederates were executed. Seif al-Islam Ibrahim was arrested but was later released; he died in uncertain circumstances soon after his return to Sana. The new Imam appointed Ahmad al-Hilali as Prime Minister and Ragheb Bey to his old post of Foreign Minister; Seiyid Husein ibn Ali al-Hilali was later appointed chief of the Royal Cabinet. Some opposition to Imam Ahmad continued to exist in some parts of the country after the middle of May, but presented no serious threat to security. When the Arab League Political Committee met to consider its recognition of the new Imam, Ibn Saud was careful not to acknowledge Ahmad until the Committee's findings were published. When it did decide to recognise Ahmad as Imam, the Committee expressed the hope that 'magnanimity would be shown to all who had opposed him' and promised that the League would 'offer all aid to achieve reform'. The Committee members who left Suez eleven days after Yahya's murder to see things for themselves never reached the Yemen; they had to observe the situation from Riyadh where they remained at the suggestion of the Amir Faisal. At the beginning of March both King Abdullah of Jordan and Seif al-Islam Abdullah pledged their support for Imam Ahmad.

At the beginning of May the new Imam established himself at Taizz, where he was visited by a Saudi Arabian delegation seeking the settlement of an old territorial dispute, and Seif al-Islam Hasan, Imam Yahya's third son, deputised for him at Sana. Seif al-Islam Ibrahim, the ninth son, was again a prisoner in the hands of the Imam and shortly to die, while Seif al-Islam Ismail, the tenth son, Seif al-Islam Qasim, the sixth, and Seif al-Islam Yahya, the twelfth, had been released from captivity by Al-Wazir's followers. Seif al-Islam Ismail on his release was imprisoned by the new Imam; Seif al-Islam Qasim, who had previously been Minister of Health, was appointed the new Minister of Communications and Seif al-Islam Yahya swore allegiance to the new Imam. Seif al-Islam Abdullah, the seventh son, who became the new Prime Minister, thought that the Muslim Brotherhood was concerned in the plot to prevent the accession of his brother Ahmad because two of the Brotherhood's leaders were in the Yemen early in the year – they had since been arrested. Four days after Ahmad made his formal entry to Sana, Seif al-Islam Abdullah went to Cairo and talked with King Farouk on March 18. On April 14, Seiyid Hasan Ibrahim, who had been appointed as the Yemen's delegate to the United Nations, left for New York. A week later the Arab League passed a resolution recognising Ahmad as Imam; and on the next day he received a congratulatory telegram from King Farouk and the governments of Great Britain, France, Holland, Italy, the United States, India and Pakistan officially recognised the new King of the Yemen. It was inevitable that Great Britain should be blamed for the upheaval that had taken place in the Yemen. One Egyptian newspaper said that 'Britain will intervene and use Ahmad as a catspaw to achieve her imperialistic ambitions.

After Imam Yahya's death a greater number of Yemenis started travelling abroad in support of Imam Ahmad in his efforts to develop the Yemen; but foreigners were still not universally welcome in the country. The Imam continued to reside at Taizz, not only because he preferred the climate there to that of Sana but because at that time he could not be sure of the loyalty of the northern tribes – who had always believed that Sana was pillaged by his orders in 1948. In addition, he was able from Taizz to keep a firm hand on the southern tribes, who would almost certainly have created trouble had he not been in the vicinity. He also believed that the southern tribes had a strong inclination to form a Shafei confederation with the tribes of the Western Aden Protectorate. Soon after Ahmad's accession, the question of his successor was raised, because most of the Imam's brothers lived in Sana where one of them, Seif al-Islam Hasan, who later went to live abroad, had a particularly strong political party behind him. Hasan, who was once Minister of Education, was an aspirant for the title of Crown Prince, but the Imam was determined that his own son Seif al-Islam al-Badr should be recognised as heir to the throne.

(ii) THE JEWS IN THE YEMEN

In the meantime, the announcement in the United Nations on November 30, 1947, of the decision to partition Palestine gave rise to severe anti-Jewish disturbances in Aden. Many Yemenite Jews, staying there temporarily before emigrating to Palestine, were killed or wounded. There were at that time possibly some 60,000 Jews in the Yemen, their community having existed in South-western Arabia for centuries before the rise of Islam.

Although living in isolated towns in the Yemen as well as on the coast and in the capital, the Yemenite Jews had rarely been out of touch with Palestine. In the third century AD, the Jews of Sana used to send their important dead to be buried in Palestine and, later, priests from Tiberias went to the Yemen to act as advisers to the king, Dhu Nowas. Further visits from Palestinian Jews took place in the ninth and tenth centuries and, in the sixteenth century, a printer from Safed in Palestine travelled in the Yemen carrying books for the Yemenite Jews to copy. In 1730 two travelling scholars, collecting money and selling books in the Yemen for the rabbinical colleges in Jerusalem, were able to inform the Yemenite Jews of the latest news from their Holy Land. The

Jewish Christian missionary Henry Aaron Stern travelled to Sana via Bajil and Menakha in 1836 and, after staying at Sana for a time, went down to the coast at Hodeida and thence to Mocha where a German–Jewish trader named Landon nursed him through a severe fever.

Ya'akov Saphir, a Jerusalem Rabbi who travelled in the Yemen in 1858 and 1859 with the object of searching for the ten lost tribes of Israel, visited many Jewish settlements in spite of being imprisoned for a time at Raudha. Saphir's two volumes of his travels, *Even Saphir*, which were published in Hebrew in 1866 and 1876 aroused a great interest among the Jewish people of Palestine in the ancient Jewish communities of the Yemen and, after 1882, when a group of Yemenite Jewish artisans reached Jerusalem, a steady immigration followed. In Aden Saphir found about 300 Yemenite Jewish families which had fled from Mocha. He found the Jews of Sana living in gloomy, cave-like dwellings. Muslims had the power of life and death over Jews, and could confiscate their property with impunity. Jews were forbidden to wear white, red or green clothing and the rich Jews had to put on the appearance of wretchedness so as not to arouse envy and so be plundered. The Jews of the Yemen were reduced to a lowly estate indeed, persecuted as they were by a people that regarded itself as holy and intensely pious. When Siegfried Langer, a young Austrian Jew, was at Madab near Sana in 1882, the Jews there told him of their knowledge of Jerusalem and of the great Rothschild whom they believed to be a great Rabbi of the Jews. They were under the illusion that Rothschild lived in Jerusalem and had bought land in the area which he was going to give to them. On the strength of this rumour, more than a hundred Jewish families from Sana travelled to Jerusalem to take advantage of it. Langer, who had stayed in Sana, was murdered at the age of 25 while on an excursion from the capital in 1882.

Yomtob Zemach, who visited the Yemen in 1910 on behalf of the Alliance Israëlite Universelle, found the 3,000 Jews in Sana suffering from the effects of the revolts of Imam Yahya against the Turks. At this time the Palestine office of the Zionist Organisation decided to send Shmuel Yavneeli to the Yemen in the disguise of a religious emissary. Yavneeli, until as late as 1955, was one of the outstanding figures of the Jewish labour movement, and the object of this visit was to tell the Jews of the great colonisation work which was going forward in Palestine, to inquire into their conditions of living and to persuade them all to emigrate. His wanderings, which are not well known, are worth recording. Setting out from Aden he took the Lahej, Dhala, Qataba route to Mawiya and Taizz, and then went on to Udain via Dhu Safil. From Udain he travelled south-west to Badan, then east through Dhu Safil again and on through Qibili to Ibb. Instead of taking the normal route from Ibb to Yerim via Mekhada and Arba al-Qala to the north, he crossed Jebel Manar to the east and visited Sadda. From there he struck north to Yerim and reached Sana via the Dhamar, Ma'han, Wa'lan track. At Dhamar Yavneeli found at least 150 Jewish families and, while based at Sana, he visited Amran and Shiham to the north-west, finally leaving the country by the Menakha–Bajil–Hodeida road. He returned to Aden, later landed on the coast to the east at Shuqra and from there he journeyed north to Al Beidha in the extreme south-east of the Yemen. From Al Beidha he visited the area of Suwadi village on the Radfan plateau to the west, without actually entering it, and then made his way to Sauma in the east. Leaving the Yemen he struck east over the Aulaqi plateau to Wasita and Habban, finally returning to Shuqra through Mahfad and Ahwar. Yavneeli was robbed and accused of being a Christian spy and finally was forced to leave the country. However, his mission was highly successful and about 15,000 Jews followed him from the Yemen to Palestine in 1911–12, the majority of them settling on the land. They formed the nucleus of a great number of flourishing agricultural settlements in what is now Israel. After the end of the Second World War, American philanthropic and other pressures were instrumental in arranging, at some discomfiture to the Aden authorities, for a gradual, and, finally in 1949, a mass exodus of Jews from the Yemen.

The emigration of Yemenite Jews was stimulated indirectly by the recrudescence in 1942 of a dormant typhus epidemic; it raged until the summer of 1944, when it began to subside. The virulence of the disease was aggravated by severe famine, the result of drought in 1942, and by the wholesale export of cereals occasioned by rising prices in Aden and Asir. The dearth of grain had stimulated a flourishing black market, and the trade was cornered by a few wealthy merchants bent on increasing their capital. These shortages induced a surge of anti-Jewish feeling which succeeded in forcing many of the Yemenite Jews to quit their ancestral home in an attempt to reach Palestine.

(iii) THE MAGIC CARPET

In 1942 some thousands of Yemenite Jews were lodged in a camp at Aden awaiting emigration certificates, and in that year typhus spread to this camp. Most prominent among the helpers at that time was the late Professor Kliger of the Hebrew University in Jerusalem. The decision of many to initiate the great exodus (the major part of which was to follow six years later) was taken in 1943, when the epidemic eventually spread to the Qaa-al-Yahud (Jewish quarter) in Sana. Consequently, towards the end of 1943, groups of Yemenite Jews began to arrive in the Aden Protectorate and, at the beginning of 1944, 800 arrived under the auspices of the Middle East Refugees' Relief Association. The emigrants were detained in camps at Fiyush and Lahej, drastic action being taken by the Aden authorities to prevent the spread of typhus within the Protectorate. Notwithstanding the prohibition on the entry of more emigrants, either Jew or Arab, further groups continued to penetrate the Protectorate illegally; typhus broke out in widely separated areas and, when shipping was available on the coast, emigrants were escorted up the Red Sea as quickly as possible. By the end of the Second World War, several thousands had managed to emigrate to Palestine, but in 1947 some 4,000 Jews still awaited transportation to Israel.

On hearing of the establishment of the state of Israel, many thousands of Yemenite Jews started trekking south, prompted mainly by religious motives, but also by the recent drought and the treatment which they had received in their homeland. Certainly there had always existed the well-known segregation and humiliation of the Jews during their centuries of settlement in the Yemen, but the main reason for the great exodus was their apparent belief that the Messiah had really arrived. During September and October 1949 between 25,000 and 40,000 were flown from the Royal Air Force airfield at Sheikh Othman in British and American aircraft chartered by the American Joint Distribution Committee and the Jewish Agency. Before leaving the Yemen, in addition to having to pay a poll tax, the Jews were compelled to surrender all their property or at least dispose of it

D*

at a great loss; hence, after making their own way across 300 miles of territory on foot or by donkey, they arrived at Aden destitute. They were housed in transit camps set up at Hiswa, and from there a nine-hour flight took them to Lydda at the rate of between 300 and 500 per day. Five Near East Airlines Skymasters and one Tudor aircraft were used in the operation, and about 140 people (as opposed to the normal load of 40) could be taken aboard each machine because the average weight of each adult was about 70 lbs, so emaciated were they by undernourishment. Indeed it was doubted by the Israeli authorities at the time whether the expense of the operation would be justified; whether these new members of their community would become useful citizens, even if the majority managed to survive their hereditary ailments. But the Yemenite Jews who were already long established in Palestine lived in close patriarchal groups, spurning imported socialism, and their fellows from Southern Arabia soon followed their example.

In spite of the valuable assistance given in Aden by the Director of Medical Services, Dr. E. Cochrane, the Israeli Government had many problems before it. After their initial demonstrations of piety, the newcomers to Israel soon forgot their religious fervour and found the primitive conditions in their Tel Aviv camp almost unbearable; many died soon after arrival. About a quarter of them had tropical ulcers, 40 per cent acute malaria and many were found to be suffering from trachoma or leprosy.

Up to the beginning of November 1949, the removal of the Yemenite Jews had cost the American Joint Distribution Committee £1,428,000 and by that time practically all Jews had left the Yemen. The Imam lost little by the absence of the Jews. As they took no part in the administration of the country, could not carry arms and, consequently, formed no part of the army, the departure of some 50,000 of them caused the Imam no military embarrassment, although he was loath to lose such a quantity of artisans.

(iv) THE LONDON TALKS 1950

The murder of Imam Yahya and the accession of his son Ahmad in 1948 was the turning point in Anglo–Yemeni affairs, and from that time relations grew steadily worse. Although the widening rift between the two countries was largely inevitable after the war, from which Great Britain had emerged victorious but impoverished, the so-called liberalising influences of the free Western world, the Communist bloc and the self-assertive Arab states would in any event have prompted a complete re-appraisal of Anglo–Yemeni affairs. But the attitude of Imam Ahmad did not contribute towards a friendly relationship; he continued to be antagonistic and obstructive and, while showing the utmost courtesy to all British officials with whom he did business, he was nevertheless always procrastinating and evasive. In 1948 he prevailed upon a treaty Sheikh in the Protectorate to stir up trouble in the Dhala area, and in August Sir Reginald Champion sent a force of about 600 Government Guards to restore order; whereupon the Sheikh fled to the Yemen, and the Imam gave him sanctuary, and then protested direct to the Foreign Office that the 'military expedition' to the frontier area had caused great anxiety in the Yemen.

A new ray of hope appeared in the Aden Residency later in the year when Sir Reginald Champion received an invitation from the Imam to visit him at Taizz. Following up the request of Seif al-Islam Abdullah during a visit to London in February, Sir Reginald Champion took the opportunity to reopen the question of the establishment of direct diplomatic relations. The Governor was received with great cordiality in Taizz when he arrived in November, but he was surprised to find that the Imam wished the Governor of Aden himself to be accredited as the British diplomatic representative to the Yemen. An extradition agreement was also discussed but found to be unworkable and abandoned. The British Government did, however, approve the extraordinary step of making a colonial governor one of His Majesty's diplomatic representatives to a foreign country, but when Sir Reginald Champion communicated this decision to the Imam in February 1949 Ahmad replied that he had now decided to postpone the matter indefinitely and to leave things as they were. The Foreign Office were of course more than a little upset at the rebuff and the subject was not raised again for more than a year.

Meanwhile on the frontier there were more immediate problems. In February 1949, following a revolt of the Rassassi tribe in the southern Yemen against the Imam's rule, Royal Air Force aircraft from Khormaksar demolished forts along the frontier. Although many of the rebels escaped into Protectorate territory, the Imam quelled the revolt and beheaded thirty-three of the ringleaders.

During the preceding March the Sherif of Beihan, wishing to put a stop to the smuggling of hides, coffee and *qat* into his territory, had asked for a frontier customs post to be set up at Nagd Margad, thirty miles north-west of Beihan and three miles from the border between Wadi Harib and Wadi Beihan. On the Governor's orders the post was built and immediately strong protests were launched by the Yemeni Government, by Qadhi Muhamad Al-Shami, the Governor of Beidha Province, and also by the Yemeni Frontier Officer who claimed that Nagd Margad was in *his* territory. Consequently, when on several occasions in early August the site of the customs post was attacked, the local British garrison defended it and for two months a regular fusillade continued. By August 14 the Yemenis, in accordance with the time-honoured strategy of these parts, had begun to build a fort within their enemy's territory at Jebel Manawa, about one mile distant from Nagd Margad. As protests from the British Agent, Major Basil Seager, were of no avail, the Acting Governor took up the matter personally with the Imam. However, no satisfactory reply was received; the fort at Jebel Manawa continued to be built and the Yemeni attacks were maintained. A reconnaisance by an Anson aircraft on August 20 established that there was little or no activity, although the building of the Yemeni fort seemed to be still in progress; ten days later the Imam was informed that unless his men withdrew behind the frontier by dawn on September 2 the Royal Air Force would take positive action. The next week leaflets were dropped on the fort calling on the garrison to withdraw, but the request was ignored and after smoke bombs had been dropped in the vicinity as a further warning, which was also disregarded, Tempest aircraft attacked and completely destroyed the fort with rocket projectiles on September 2. When the bombs were dropped the Yemeni garrison, estimated at about twenty men, withdrew and although it reappeared when the aircraft returned to base, the Yemenis returned to their own territory after the fort had been demolished. One Yemeni was severely wounded – apparently the only casualty.

On September 8, 1949, an official of the Yemeni Foreign Office lodged at the British Embassy in Egypt a written protest against the action of the Royal Air Force, and the matter was reported to the Arab League, with whose assistance the Yemen intended to appeal to the UN Security Council unless it could obtain financial compensation. His Majesty's Government received much adverse criticism in Egypt, the main line of attack being that Great Britain was attempting to exert pressure on the Yemen in order to procure the oil rights at Shabwa; this criticism was prompted by the visit of an oil exploration party of Petroleum Concessions Ltd. to Shabwa in November 1949. In a public declaration on September 11, the Imam accused Great Britain of 'attacking Yemeni independence and dignity' in that fourteen Royal Air Force aircraft had bombed and caused casualties to 'peaceful inhabitants in the Harib area, doing much damage to property'. After summoning his advisers the Imam instructed his Foreign Minister, then in Paris, to prepare an appeal to the Security Council. In the last week of September, the four Yemeni delegates at Flushing Meadows went to lay their case before the United Nations. The thesis of the protest, as quoted by Seiyid Abdullah al-Amri, was that Great Britain had violated the United Nations' charter by attacking another member. In the meantime Sir Reginald Champion had tried to alleviate matters by writing to the Imam on September 29 suggesting that boundary pillars should be erected along the frontier in order to avoid further disputes and in December he tried to arrange a meeting between his and the Imam's officials to decide upon the 1934 *status quo* line. Both of these approaches failed.

The outcome of the reference to the United Nations of the dispute, by now known as the 'Beihan incident', was a decision that the two governments should negotiate together to find their own solution to the problem, and early in 1950 Al-Amri came to England to discuss the old question of diplomatic representatives and to protest once again at the Beihan incident. He returned to Cairo without any agreement having been reached. Later, his government asked the Foreign Office if talks could begin in London on June 20 but on July 10 the Foreign Office suddenly announced that it was Great Britain that had called the conference to demonstrate its willingness 'to seek with the government of the Yemen a settlement of all outstanding differences'. The four points which were to provide the basis of the agenda were as follows:

1, the settlement of the frontier dispute arising out of the Beihan incident and a definition of the southern frontier of the Yemen;

2, the settlement of the question of diplomatic relations;

3, a decision regarding Yemeni complaints about the Shabwa area; and

4, the improvement of commercial relations.

The talks were scheduled to start in the week beginning August 28. In the second week of August, Al-Amri, Seiyid Hasan Ibrahim (Minister of State) and Qadhi Muhamad Al-Shami, en route to London, arrived in Cairo where they were welcomed by the Egyptian Foreign Minister, Dr. Muhamad Saleh al-Din Bey, who later met them at the Cairo suburb of Bulkeley on August 25 to hear the views which they were to put forward at the forthcoming meeting in London. The Egyptian Government had already agreed to lend the services of Dr. Hasan Bughadi Bey as adviser to the delegation in London.

In London G. W. Furlonge, head of the Eastern Department of the Foreign Office, was appointed chairman of the meeting and two Colonial Office officials with long experience of Anglo–Yemeni relations represented the British point of view. Of these one was Sir Reginald Champion, who flew from Aden on August 23 and immediately attended meetings at the Foreign and Colonial Offices; the other was Colonel Sir Bernard Reilly of the Colonial Office, who welcomed the Yemeni delegation on its arrival in London. Long before the talks began it was expected that the conference would not agree a final settlement, but rather a *modus vivendi* whereby further frontier incidents might be avoided. It was also believed, optimistically, that the trade talks besides being informal might be followed by a 'full scale pact'. There were high hopes for the talks on both sides and, even by the second week in October, when the talks were still in progress, there was every indication that both delegations were prepared to take their time in resolving the problems before them. Al-Amri helped to create goodwill by not pressing his country's claim for compensation for the Beihan incident, although he was clearly anxious, when the meeting began, to extract a promise from Great Britain that air attacks on the Yemen would stop. He was also keen that London and Sana should exchange diplomatic representatives, preferably at ministerial level, making it plain that he had long been dissatisfied with the procedure whereby all diplomatic questions had been conducted through the Aden Government; and he made his views

known to the British Foreign Secretary, Ernest Bevin, when he
called on him on August 30. Al-Amri was well liked by the
British negotiating team, and made a generally good impression
in London during his visit; when the talks ended on October 10,
it was apparent that they had in fact been most friendly, both
delegations agreeing upon proposals for the settling of the frontier
dispute and the exchange of diplomatic representatives before the
end of the year. These proposals were to be referred to the respective governments to be ratified before publication. 'Technical
co-operation', a subject discussed, was not on the original published
agenda as such, but the Yemeni Government was offered the
services of the British Middle East Office in Cairo for assistance
with matters such as irrigation, agriculture, public works, medicine
and hygiene. It was agreed that proposals should be made to each
government for the setting up of a Boundary Commission to
examine the ground of previous frontier disputes so that there
could be a permanent delimitation of the Aden–Yemen border;
in the meantime, neither government was to take any action which
would disturb the *status quo*. It was agreed as a corollary that neither
government would undertake any subversive propaganda against
the other pending ratification of the conference's proposals. The
informal trade talks had little result and it is difficult to understand
what could have been the basis of any 'full scale trade pact'. Most
of the British trade carried out with the Yemen was conducted
at that time between Hodeida and Aden, and the Imam himself
controlled all trade between the territories. He owned the only
dhow carrying merchandise between the two ports; no other ships
might carry merchandise from Hodeida and vessels bringing
goods into the port had to leave with empty holds.

After the conference Al-Amri was confident that direct diplomatic relations would be established and when Dr. Hasan Bughadi
Bey returned to Egypt he was also full of high hopes. (At the meeting he had only given his opinion on technical matters as they
arose, and confined his participation in political questions to
statements of fact.) Early in December it was decided by the
Yemeni government that Qadhi Muhamad Mahmoud al-Zubayri,
who had led the Yemeni Delegation to the United Nations Social
Studies Seminar in Cairo in 1950, would be appointed Chargé
d'Affaires of the new Yemeni Legation in London but, when the
actual appointment came to be made, it was not he who was chosen.

6

THE BEGINNING OF THE END

(i) DIPLOMATIC REPRESENTATION 1951

Al-Amri's confidence in the forthcoming establishment of diplomatic relations was not widely shared among those who were well acquainted with Anglo-Yemeni affairs. The news of the ratification of the agreement was therefore received by the British Government with some surprise. Al-Amri returned to London just after the middle of January 1951, notes of ratification were exchanged on the 20th, and at the end of the month Al-Amri was on his way back to Hodeida from Cairo. In August the Minister of State, Seiyid Hasan Ibrahim, who had been a member of the 1950 delegation to London, was designated the first Yemeni Minister to the Court of St. James and during August and September he made some preliminary arrangements for the assumption of his duties. He paid a formal visit to Mr. Kenneth Younger, the British Minister of State in August, but he could not present his credentials formally to King George VI, owing to His Majesty's illness, until some time later. In October, Michael Jacomb left England for Sana to take up his duties as Chargé d'Affaires in the Yemen, with the distinction of being the first British diplomatic representative to be accredited to any government of the Kingdom of Yemen but the hopes of setting up a frontier commission were never realised, and the 1951 agreement soon faded into oblivion.

The abrogation by Egypt in 1952 of the Anglo-Egyptian Treaty of 1936 gave the Yemen an opportunity to show that, in spite of these moves towards an Anglo-Yemeni settlement, it would still continue to support the major Arab League members. On November 13, 1951, Egypt's second 'National Struggle Day', Seiyid Ali al-Moayyad followed the lead of all other Arab countries' diplomatic representatives in Cairo by publicly announcing that 'the Yemen gives its blessing to Egypt in its struggle and condems the action of the English'. Earlier, when the Arab League had met to discuss the Four Power proposals for a Middle East Command, Sheikh al-Gaabary, the Yemeni delegate, was among those who opposed the plan. During 1951, however, British–Yemeni relations remained good on the surface but, in February 1952, the Yemen was one of the Arab countries which signed the Arab Defence Pact, and soon afterwards there were difficulties between the two countries once more. In April 1952 Fadhl Abdul Karim, Sultan of Lahej, was asked by the Aden authorities to come to Aden during an inquiry into the deaths of two of his cousins, Amir Hassan Ali and Amir Ahmad Mahdi. The Aden Government believed that the Sultan's presence in Lahej during the inquiry would be undesirable and he fled instead to the Yemen. Road and telephone communications between Lahej and Aden were cut, Lahej was occupied by the Aden Levies and a Council of Regency was soon set up in Sultanate by the Aden Government on April 24. Just over a month later the Sultan's younger brother, Ali Abdul Karim, aged 28, succeeded to the Sultanate and took over the reins of power from the Regency Council.

The Yemen Government seemed agitated by this move, and the Legation in London expressed its astonishment at the British action. 'Any measure', it declared, 'must adhere to the letter and spirit of the treaties concluded between Her Majesty's Government and the Yemen Government and between Her Majesty's Government and the Sultan of Lahej.' The events which led to the taking over of security in Lahej probably began in 1932 when the Sultan lost an eye in an assassination attempt, since which time, and particularly after 1947 when he succeeded his father as ruler, he had seemed to be suffering from persecution mania, seeing possible usurpers of his throne everywhere. In 1951 he had banished his brother, Ali, and most of his cousins to Aden.

(ii) ADEN'S EARLY FEDERATION PLANS

The Second World War had delayed any follow-up action by the Aden Government after it had managed to secure a relative peace in the Protectorate. Two Advisory Treaties had been signed with Eastern Protectorate rulers before the war, and in 1944 and 1945 five Western Protectorate rulers signed similar treaties. These were the rulers of the Fadhli, Lower Aulaqi, Lower Yafai, Beihan and Dhala, and in 1951 the Upper Aulaqi, Audhali and Lahej rulers joined their ranks. Already in that year the first plans for a federation of Western Aden Protectorate rulers had been sent to London by the Aden Governor; and late in January 1954 the first Federation proposals were put to the rulers and accepted in principle. These steps toward consolidation of British power in the protectorates caused the Imam to intensify his campaign of subversion in the British sphere; from the beginning of 1952, by means of bribery, hostage taking and gun running, he was taking positive steps to stir up as much trouble as he could. In December 1952 he ordered his Governor of Beidha to imprison the Upper Yafai Sultan and it was only by means of the withdrawal of permission for Yemeni civil aircraft to land at Aden that the Sultan came to be released after two months.

In January the next year about 800 Subeihi tribesmen from the Aden Protectorate fled across the frontier into the Yemen after refusing to pay local taxes, and after opposing a British force which was sent to restore order. Then a small detachment of troops from the Sultanate of Lahej was sent to arrest Sheikh Muhamad Shaher of the Subeihi, who was stirring up his tribesmen against Lahej land and fishery taxes; the detachment was driven off with one killed, and Sheikh Shaher took refuge with Mansuri tribesmen. As for the 800 Subeihi tribesmen, they took refuge in Qubaita, a district of the Yemen under the leadership of Sheikh Mansuri and Sheikh Shaher. The Yemen, it appeared, was prepared to let the insurgent tribesmen organise resistance to the Aden Government from the safety of its own territory and to supply them with arms and ammunition. However, the Sultan of Lahej's troops had subdued them before the end of the month.

In the following year there were more frontier incidents. Between May 1 and 24, 1954, about twenty-eight raids were made on the Protectorate from the Yemen, and Yemeni raiders attacked Mukeiras on June 10. A week later a serious attack was made on Martea by about eighty regular Yemeni troops and 400 tribal irregulars. At the beginning of July Great Britain threatened direct action if the Yemeni Government did not take some positive steps to prevent these frontier attacks. Seiyid Hasan Ibrahim, the Yemeni Chargé d'Affaires in London, was called to the Foreign Office and handed a note in which his Government's attention was drawn to the serious situation which continued to exist on the Aden–Yemen frontier. In addition to detailing the recent incidents, the Note said that the Yemen continued to foment rebellion in the Protectorate and to give encouragement, money and arms to lawless elements such as the Dammani, the Rabizi and the Hassani Akil. The actions of the Yemeni Government, said the Note, gave colour to the belief that it laid claim to the whole of the Aden Protectorate and had no intention of settling the frontier problem. Any such claim was firmly rejected by Great Britain who asked the Yemen Government to stop not only the attacks mounted from its own territory but also the supply of arms, money and food to Protectorate tribes. Yemen Government's reply protested that flights by RAF aircraft over Yemeni territory were open acts of provocation, and continued:

> The flights are made over houses from a low height, thus frightening peaceful women and children in their homes. Such acts cannot be described except as open acts of provocation and an infringement of all the provisions of both public and private international agreements. Furthermore, these acts took place at a time when the Government of HM the Imam were endeavouring to meet the recently agreed-upon suggestion of the British Government to hold a meeting with a view to eliminating all the causes of the incidents which originated from the attacks made against the Yemen guard-points by Aden forces.

It was widely thought in the British press that the visit to the Yemen of Major Saleh Salem (the most prominent of the anti-British politicians in the Egyptian Government at that time) just before the exchange of notes, had given great impetus to the actions of the Yemeni Government. The Egyptian newspaper *Akhbar al-Yom* of July 10 said that Major Salem had visited the scene of the 'latest British aggression' during the first week in July, and inspected 'ruined houses and encouraged people who resisted British attack'. It was also announced at this time that an Egyptian military mission would be sent to the Yemen to 'train the Yemeni Army in modern warfare by the introduction of artillery, planes and tanks'.

Frontier incidents are often used to divert attention from more serious domestic situations inside the Yemen; however the main reason for the Yemen's quarrel with Britain at this time was supposedly the British plan to create a Federation of the Western Aden Protectorate states. The Imam saw in the scheme a strengthening and consolidation of those Shafai states south of their frontier who might well ally themselves against the Zeidi ruling minority in the Yemen with the southern Shafai. Great Britain, when rejecting the Yemeni Note, said that RAF aircraft had not flown low over Beidha 'in open acts of aggression'. British civil aircraft circling to land at Mukeiras might have passed near Beidha, but had not flown over it, and in any case landings such as these had been made for many years. Further frontier raids were made by Yemeni tribesmen in September and October, although in early September the Political Committee of the Arab League had already decided that it would still seek a peaceful solution of the Aden–Yemen frontier dispute through diplomatic channels.

At the end of July 1954, it became clear that Imam Ahmad's position was being threatened by some of his own countrymen. Seif al-Islam al-Hasan, the Imam's eldest brother, and Seif al-Islam Muhamad al-Badr, his twenty-seven-year-old son, were the main contestants for the throne in addition to Seif al-Islam Abdullah, another of the Imam's brothers. However, peace prevailed for a time and the Imam retained his throne at Taizz. This was not the first attempt made to overthrow the régime: in February 1950 Seif al-Islam Ismail, a brother of the Imam, had been arrested at Hajja for preparing a revolt against him. But early in April 1955 an attempt was made to depose the Imam Ahmad by Seif al-Islam Abdullah, at the head of a section of the Army. There was a clash with the royal bodyguard near Taizz, and 600 soldiers marched on the town, besieging the Imam in his palace for several days. The rebels demanded his abdication in favour of Seif al-Islam Abdullah, Ahmad agreeing to surrender his executive power but not his position as Imam. By this means he soon won over some of the rebels and there was fighting near Taizz, where most of the townsmen rallied to the Imam's cause. Muhamad al-Badr, his son, now managed to escape to Hajja where, after rallying about 30,000 troops and tribesmen he marched on Taizz and occupied it on April 5, having routed the rebels and restored his father to the throne. Five days later al-Badr was proclaimed heir to the throne. Seif al-Islam Abdullah and Seif al-Islam Abbas (another brother of the Imam) tried to flee the country but were arrested, tried for treason and executed on April 13, their bodies being publicly exposed before burial.

Lieutenant-Colonel Ahmad Thalayee, the chief army instructor and leader of the revolt, and five others were also executed. When news of the revolt reached Cairo, an Egyptian mission, led by Lieutenant-Colonel Shafei (Minister of Social Affairs), as well as officials from Saudi Arabia, flew to Taizz on April 3 to try to reconcile the two sides. Imam Ahmad gave the Mission an assurance that he would open up his country in complete co-operation with Saudi Arabia and Egypt, in exchange for promises of help from those countries against Britain.

Anglo-Yemeni relations continued to deteriorate in 1954 and 1955, in spite of a visit to the Imam at Taizz by Sir Tom Hickin-botham, Governor of Aden, in October 1954. Yemeni suspicions over the acceptance of the principle of federation by the Sheikh-doms of the Western Aden Protectorate; the right claimed by the Yemen under the treaty of Sana that the *status quo* should apply to the territory south of the frontier in addition to the frontier itself; and the fear that the Shafai states of the Protectorate would unite with the Shafais of the Yemen to overthrow the Zeidi Imamate, were all contributory causes of the frontier incidents between 1951 and 1957.

(iii) THE BASIS OF THE FRONTIER PROBLEM

The operations of the Anglo-Turkish Boundary Commission had begun in 1902 at Sheikh Said, and by 1904 it had agreed upon a frontier line as far as a point near the Wadi Bana just north-north-east of Qataba. As the Turks could not control the tribes in the areas to the east, a straight line was drawn on the map at an angle of 45 degrees from that point and this was agreed as the continuation of the division between Turkish and British spheres of influence. This part of the Anglo-Turkish Commission frontier was known (due to esoteric cartographic reasons) as the Violet Line. This whole frontier line as agreed by the Anglo-Turkish Commission was ratified in 1914 by the Anglo-Turkish Convention. After 1919 the Imam encroached into the British sphere but, at the time of the signature of the Treaty of Sana in 1934, he had retired behind the whole of the Anglo-Turkish line with the exception of a 'bulge' made in the Violet Line caused by his continued occupation since 1923 of the Sultanate of Beidha. Because the Rassasi tribe, which occupied this area, was not in treaty relations with Aden (the Indian Government of the time would not grant the money for a subsidy) the British did not press their claim to Beidha; the *status quo* of the Treaty of Sana referred in British eyes to the whole of the Anglo–Turkish line with the exception of the bulge in the Violet Line, which they conceded.

The Treaty of Sana laid down that the 'situation existing in regard to the frontier' in February 1934 should be maintained for the future and that neither country should interfere with the inhabitants of the other's area of influence. Imam Yahya observed the treaty within reasonable limits, and although, as sovereign of a successor state of the Turkish Empire, he was obliged to by international law, he had never recognised the Anglo–Turkish Convention of 1914 and in the Treaty of Sana care was taken to avoid any mention of it. As early as 1926 Clayton had found that the Imam Yahya claimed the whole of South-west Arabia including Aden Colony, and the Imam Ahmad, and later his son also, were to revive this claim. Ahmad based his claims on the surmise that the Arabic word interpreted as 'frontier' in the Treaty of Sana did in fact mean not a border line, but 'frontier areas,' or the areas between the Yemen and the British spheres – undetermined areas on either side of the supposed frontier and especially on the British side. Thus he said that any change in the internal administration – military, civil or economic – in the Protectorates from that existing in 1934 was a violation of the Treaty of Sana. When it suited them, successive Imams chose to declare that the *status quo* referred not to changes in the frontier line but to anything that changed the way of life in the protectorate – even to the building of a frontier post. Conditions in his territory were allowed to alter, but not those in the Protectorate.

Pacification of the Protectorate could be carried on from Aden from 1934 to 1939, and the Advisory Treaty system was developed from 1945 to 1954. (By this system, a state promised to keep the peace in exchange for a subsidy, and to allow a British Adviser to reside in the territory, his advice to be accepted and acted upon.) From 1954 onwards the Federation scheme began to take root. These three lines of progress were successful because the Protectorate tribes, being of the Shafai persuasion, preferred British influence to domination by the Shia Imams. Consolidation of Shafai Protectorate tribes was a threat to the Shia Imams in the Yemen, where the majority of the tribesmen were Shafai, who

might well side with their co-religionists in the Protectorate to
overthrow the Imamate.

(iv) HICKINBOTHAM'S FEDERATION PLANS

During the period of internal trouble in the Yemen in the first
half of 1955 the frontier remained comparatively quiet, but as
high summer approached more attacks were made in the Beihan
area. In the Western Aden Protectorate two British officers and
ten native soldiers were killed in June 1955 when Rabizi tribesmen
ambushed a convoy. A battalion of Seaforth Highlanders and a
motorised squadron of the Life Guards were flown in to the area,
the Colonial Office announcing in August that this and other
disturbances had been fomented by the Yemen. The Egyptian
Government was not slow to make political capital out of the
increasing tension on the Aden–Yemen border. In early March
1956, Colonel Nasser made it clear to King Saud and President
Kuwatly of Syria that to Egypt it was of the utmost importance to
consolidate Arab interests on the Red Sea and Indian Ocean where
foreign influence 'may always jeopardise the military economic
and political independence of the Arabs in the hinterlands.'
Complete liberation of these points from imperialist domination
was one of the objects of Egypt's policy.

For some time now Aden had been beset by labour unrest and
a series of politically inspired strikes, engineered and encouraged
by Egyptain propaganda. In mid-March one of the eleven Balhareth
sheikhs was bought over by the Yemenis for 50,000 riyals, and
some 600 Saudi rifles were sent to Marib in Saudi trucks for
distribution among the Protectorate tribes. In April 1956 the
Yemen signed a military pact with Egypt, Syria and Saudi Arabia.

Colonel Nasser's anti-British campaign in South-western
Arabia did not deter Sir Tom Hickinbotham from holding a
conference on March 31 with eighteen Western Aden Protectorate
rulers to discuss the Federation plan. The Government of Aden
had made the initial proposal in 1953 and by 1954 most of the
rulers had agreed to it in principle. In some quarters it was criticised
as being over complicated and calculated to alarm those who were
invited to participate. After the conference the following statement
was issued:

The Governor recently held conversations with the rulers of

the Aden Protectorate with the object of discussing with them the long-term future of the states of the Protectorate. It is the policy of Her Majesty's Government in the Protectorate, as elsewhere, to guide and assist all dependent territories towards maximum political and economic development which the circumstances of each may warrant. Her Majesty's Government sympathises with the view that individually the States of the Aden Protectorate are too small in area, population, and resources to be able to become economically and politically fully developed, and that therefore they should seek some form of close association with each other for mutual assistance and support in order to strengthen their internal economy and social organisation.

The rulers and peoples of these States are entirely free to negotiate among themselves, with such advice of Her Majesty's Government as they may require, such form of closer association as may suit them best, and which in due course will enable them to benefit by the declared policy of Her Majesty's Government.

They shall further have complete freedom among themselves to choose or reject any proposals that may be made for the attainment of the objective of closer association. Her Majesty's Government will afford to any consequent combination of States assistance and protection similar to that which they now afford and will continue to afford to individual States of the Protectorate.

The Sheikhs in their turn issued the following statement to the Government of Aden through the Sultan of Lahej, who was acting on their behalf:

We, the Rulers of the Sultanates and Amirates of South Arabia who are gathered in Aden, appreciate the fine spirit of Her Majesty's Government which prompted the announcement on March 31, 1956, regarding Her Majesty's Government's policy towards our countries and their future.

We believe that the development and progress of our countries in the future depends on close association and co-operation between them. We believe from the statement of Her Majesty's Government that their policy in our countries is to help to develop them to the maximum degree, both politically and economically; further, that the Rulers of these States and their people have complete freedom to negotiate among themselves the appropriate form which this association and co-operation should take, and that they have complete freedom to choose or reject suggestions which may be put to them.

All this had made a profound impression on us, and the enunciation of these principles will increase our confidence in and will strengthen the friendship between us and Her Majesty's Government. We, the Chiefs of the Sultanates and Amirates, feel that the discussions which will take place to consider co-operation and association with a view to reaching a more acceptable organisation of our countries should be in accordance with the public spirit which is crystallised and developed in the aims and objects of Arab nationalism.

We pray God that He will guide us for the best and direct our steps to the attainment of our desires.

While the strikes in Aden continued well into May 1956, Colonel Nasser met the Imam Ahmad and King Saud at Jedda on April 21, to discuss methods of fomenting further unrest in the Protectorate, and against the 'British seizure' of Kamaran where the British Petroleum Company was operating; also to arrange for the Yemen's adherence to the Egypt–Syria–Saudi military pact. (The Yemen had already protested officially at the end of January 1956 against the granting of the concession by the British Government for oil exploration on Kamaran Island). The pact was signed shortly after Russia's declaration that she would work for an Arab–Israel peace settlement. In the generally anti-British atmosphere which prevailed at the time, *Al Anba* (Damascus) noted that both Eastern and Western Powers 'help us only when it is in their interests to do so'. *Al Ittihad* (Damascus) claimed that Russia helped the Arabs only to 'get the best out of the cold war with the Western Powers'. The Jedda Pact (as it came to be called) was hailed by *Al Gomhouria* (Cairo), which said that the Red Sea basin now came 'under complete control of the Arab front', while *Al Akhbar* (Cairo) declared that the pact would now 'hinder Britain from hatching intrigues in the Arab peninsula'.

Frontier incidents continued. On April 7 a Government Guard

post in Wadi Khaura in the Upper Aulaqi Sultanate was attacked
and it was again fired upon two nights later when two Seijani
tribesmen tried to force their way into the post after killing a
sentry. Tribesmen later fired on the post from surrounding villages
and plantations but Government Guards, helped by RAF aircraft,
then attacked, killing two more of the raiders and wounding four.
Some members of the Ahl Abdullah and Ahl Saleh sections of the
Seijani tribe who refused to pay the Aden Government a sub-
sequent fine of 4,000 riyals had their houses burned down as a
punishment. A large force of Yemenis crossed the frontier at this
time and attacked Aden Government guards at Manawa in the
Emir of Beihan's territory; firing continued for some hours but
there were no casualties. At the beginning of May RAF aircraft
were sent to Khaura Fort to scatter attacking tribesmen with
cannon fire and rockets. Saudi rifles continued to be supplied to
the Protectorate tribes. On May 20, 115 tribesmen were captured
when returning from Saudi territory in three trucks with gifts
of rifles and taken to Fort Husn al-Abr on the Yemen frontier.
A week later there were skirmishes and exchanges of fire near the
fort and a Lincoln and four Venom aircraft opened fire on the
sixty Seiar tribesmen who had collected in the area.

During the next month there were some diplomatic exchanges.
On July 13, 1956, the Yemeni Chargé d'Affaires in London protested to the Foreign Office against the 'massing of British troops'
near a customs post between Harib and Beihan. He claimed that
the force consisted of 200 soldiers, two tanks, twelve vehicles and
six guns. Neither the Foreign Office nor the Colonial Office knew
anything of these 'troop movements'. Investigation of two
similar Yemeni protests in June showed that Aden Protectorate
patrols had been in action expelling Yemeni tribesmen who had
been raiding huts and stealing goats. The new British Chargé
d'Affaires at Taizz, Monteith, later protested to the Yemen
Government about an incident in the Aden Protectorate in the
middle of July 1956, when Yemeni tribesmen crossed the frontier
near Mukeiras and fired on Audhali villages. Audhali tribesmen
drove them back killing two Yemenis. On July 19 the Yemeni
Chargé d'Affaires in London called at the Foreign Office to
protest against the action of RAF aircraft in flying over the Beidha
area during the action on July 14. The intervention of the RAF
he said, had 'caused great alarm among the inhabitants'.

In September 1956, more vigorous attempts were made by Egypt and the Yemen to stir up an insurrection in the Aden Protectorates. Cairo Radio and the broadcasting station at Sana, both beamed on Aden, poured forth a torrent of propaganda against the 'British Imperialists'. During the second week in September, Sana radio station broadcast a programme praising the action of those who had ambushed and killed Sheilh Darwish, who was supposed to be a British agent. These broadcasts were only the beginning of a full radio war which was to develop in the early months of 1957. Much propaganda of this type was disseminated to distract attention from internal shortcomings – such as the mutiny in the Yemen army, which took place in October 1956 because of inadequate pay and the short notice at which troops were moved to reinforce Qati on the Aden border.

(v) FRONTIER INCIDENTS 1955–7

The Yemen was quick to take advantage of Great Britain's severely damaged prestige in the Middle East following the fiasco on the Suez Canal in 1956. The frontier incidents which were to follow in 1957 were not unusual in their character except for being on a larger scale than usual, and were accompanied by a full-blooded propaganda campaign. During the first two weeks of January 1957, British military activity was not more than one-third above the normal level; the raids made by the Yemenis were certainly bolder than usual, and, as an innovation regular troops were introduced into the battles. At the end of January, the Imam invited the press of the world to visit him and members of his Government. Convoys of press correspondents passed through the firing lines across no-man's land, when temporary cease-fires were arranged for their safe conduct.

Two or three ruined houses bore testimony to the punishment inflicted in a RAF bombardment on the dissident village of Jalilah for the murder of a local holy man in August 1956. This affair set off a series of frontier incidents in 1956 and 1957 which developed into the most publicised of all the battles which have taken place on the Yemen borders. October 1956, a Russian ship docked at Salif and landed small-arms, ammunition and about fifty light anti-aircraft guns, the outcome of an arms deal with Czechoslovakia.

On Christmas Day, troops of the Protectorate security force

pursued a party of raiders across the frontier toward Qataba when they had attacked a government fort near Dhala. Shots were exchanged on the outskirts of Qataba and a few buildings were slightly damaged by small-arms fire. The Yemeni Government claimed that British forces also raided into the Yemen on December 26, injuring five women.

At the same time, while Aden and Yemeni leaders were trying to arrange a truce on December 24, following a recent frontier incident in the Beihan area, Yemeni tribesmen made an un-provoked attack on members of a Beihan tribe. The next day armed Yemeni tribesmen crossed the frontier and directed heavy fire on the houses of the Amir of Beihan and the British Agent at Dhala. This raid was driven off by local levies.

Four further attacks at various points along the frontier were made by Yemeni tribesmen between December 24 and January 1. One of these attacks was made on the village of Al-Baji, and here a woman was wounded and fifty cattle were stolen. At Idid, in Shaib, which was attached by Yemeni troops and Mureisi tribesmen, an 8-year-old girl was killed. A number of villages in the Beihan area were also attacked in addition to the fort at Ghaniya.

Further raids were made into Protectorate territory near Beihan at the beginning of 1957, and after some fierce encounters the Yemenis asked for a truce, which was granted by the Amir of Beihan on condition that the opposing tribesmen left the sur-rounding hills and withdrew across the frontier. The conditions were not fulfilled, and the Yemenis took advantage of the lull in the fighting to bring up more ammunition. Fighting broke out again; the Yemenis started building new forts on the frontier line, and there was some fierce fighting around the Naqd Meizar post near Beihan.

Mr. Monteith, the British Chargé d'Affaires in Taizz, protested to the Yemeni Government about the raids between December 30, 1956 and January 1, 1957. This was the third in what was to become a long series of protests and counter-protests by both governments. Seiyid Hasan Ibrahim, Yemeni Chargé d'Affaires in London had issued one to the Foreign Office on December 28 protesting against the incidents of December 24–25. By January 7 the Arab propaganda machine was in full cry, led by Cairo Radio and the Yemeni Legation in Bonn. Qadhi Abder-Rahman Abd er-Rabbuh Al-Baidani. Chargé d'Affaires in Bonn, announced on

January 7 that incendiary and high explosive bombs had been dropped on the Yemen, that British tanks were attacking, that several Yemeni Government and customs posts had been blown up and that 173 Yemeni patriots had been killed and a number wounded. He claimed that his 'partiots had shot down one RAF bomber near Al-Beidha on January 6, and two on the next day. Cairo Radio asserted that the 'British Imperialists are continuing their savage aggression against Saudi Arabia' and preparing for a large-scale invasion of the Yemen. Royal Air Force aircraft had in fact been in action on January 6 but inside the Protectorate boundary; they joined in the fighting in the Beihan area against Yemeni troops and rebel Aden tribesmen. Ernest Kennedy, the British Adviser (by the Advisory Treaty System), who drove to Beihan to investigate, was fired at by dissident tribesmen. Fighting continued around Dhala, Beihan and Rabiz, and the Yemeni authorities at Beidha and Harib assembled tribesmen from their neighbourhoods for an attack on Beihan.

The Yemeni Ambassador in Cairo, Seiyid Abdul Rahman Abu-Taleb, went to see Colonel Nasser on January 7 to ask for help, and on the 9th met the Soviet Ambassador, Kissilev. This talk with Nasser was widely publicised for propaganda purposes, and the British were accused of trying to occupy the area of Qataba and Al-Beidha and of occupying 'Atak international airport', a desert airstrip which is sixty miles inside Aden Protectorate territory. The Yemen decided to raise the matter before the United Nations, and the Political Committee of the Arab League on January 7 issued a resolution 'condemning British aggression'. When Seiyid Hasan Ibrahim was summoned to the Foreign Office on January 8, Derek Riches, head of the Eastern Department, handed him a note which rejected a previous Yemeni protest of January 2, and went on to say:

Mr. Selwyn Lloyd finds, however, that on December 31, 1956, a ruined site at Al-Hajar inside the Aden Protectorate was occupied by Yemeni intruders, and that RAF aircraft took action against them to disperse them. Her Majesty's Government for their part protest strongly against the action of the Yemen Government in failing to restrain their subjects from entering Aden Protectorate territory in this way. They reiterate the view which they have frequently expressed to the Yemen

Government that peaceful conditions will not be possible in the border areas unless the Yemen authorities prevent such contraventions of Article 3 of the 1934 Treaty of Friendship.

Attacks by Yemeni forces, including regular soldiers, continued. Women and children of the Shaib Sheikhdom were killed in some forays originating from Qataba, and Protectorate tribesmen had Yemenis billeted on them. Houses were burned in the Beihan area, and buildings in and around Dhala were damaged by the intruders. The people of Ahl-Murais built forts on the border under orders from Qataba and were directing their fire into the Beihani villages of Sahm al-Ardaf and Sahm al-Naqdi. Attacks continued in the Beihan area, and Venom aircraft were used to help loyal tribesmen and the local security forces drive the Yemenis back across the frontier. British troops also drove off attacks in the Dhala area.

The series of attacks at this time was believed by the Aden Government to have been instigated by the Yemeni Government to divert attention once more from internal unrest in the Eastern Yemen. Yemeni troops had been sent to the east in early January to attend to local disturbances, and the Naib of Ibb, one of the most powerful men in the country, also supported these frontier raids to conceal his own shortcomings. Heavy Yemeni reinforcements now began to arrive at Harib and a Yemeni officer at Nata asked for a truce which was granted on condition that he withdrew his men from the hills overlooking certain Beihani villages. In the Upper Aulaqi Sultanate near Nisab, dissidents in the pay of the Yemen burned crops belonging to one of the tribesmen. The villages of Jalilah and Safra, near Dhala, were fired on by members of the Qataba garrison. The organization, strength and concentration of all these attacks indicated strong grounds for suspecting foreign participation. In Bonn on January 10, Al-Baidani said that his government would appeal to the United Nations against 'British aggression', and that he welcomed the proposal (the source of which he did not mention) that an International Commission under the UN should demarcate the frontier. Recruiting centres were opened in Cairo, Damascus and Moscow for volunteers to fight on the side of the Yemen. Al-Baidani claimed that he had received several thousand applications from people in various countries offering their services. About 200 youths in the Egyptian volunteer liberation army expressed their willingness to go to the Yemen. By January 15, about 5,000 volunteers had registered in Cairo; and a number had registered in Syria and Jordan.

British troop reinforcements were flown into Aden from East Africa on January 11, the day that further attacks were made by Yemeni forces whose garrison at Qataba had been reinforced to a strength of about 900 men. Troops from Qataba attacked Bir Walah near Beihan. Attacks also came in the more usual way from dissidents from Aden Protectorate tribes living in the Yemen. About fifteen men fired into a village on Jebel Jihaf on the night of January 9, and the post of a home guard at Bilad Al-Azariq was attacked at the same time. On the same day the Yemeni Legation in Bonn issued a statement to the effect that the British in Aden were engaged in suppressing a large-scale revolt among the Protectorate tribes; it also announced that the number of dead had increased to several hundred, including ten 'foreigners' resident in the Protectorate. RAF aircraft had continued their attacks on Qataba, Harib, and Al-Beidha.

In Cairo on January 11 Abdul Rahman Abu Taleb, the Yemeni Minister, called a meeting of the 'Joint Command' of the armies of Egypt, Saudi Arabia and Yemen. On the following day the Yemeni Chargé d'Affaires in Washington, Seiyid Ahmad Ali Zabarak, made a formal appeal to the USA to 'halt British aggression'. Mr. Rountree, Assistant Secretary of State, making the surprising assumption that the United States were concerned in the dispute, promised to discuss the matter with the British authorities. On January 17 Rountree stated that 'the United States had urged and would continue to urge the greatest restraint'. Abu Taleb announced in Cairo on the following day that his Government considered the Treaty of Sana of 1934 and the Anglo-Yemeni agreement of 1951 to be abrogated. No communication on this subject was ever received at the Foreign Office in London, and on January 20 Abu Taleb, after speaking with President Nasser, said that the Yemen had 'decided not to abrogate its treaties with Britain'. Attacks by Yemenis were made on January 9 on Khalika in the Western Aden Protectorate, on January 10 on Wadi Khaura post in the Western Aden Protectorate and on January 11 on Ghaniya post near Beihan. At this time the intensity of the radio war increased, and Cairo and Sana radio stations turned their efforts to tempting Aden Levy troops to desert across the frontier.

By January 14 regular troops of the Yemen Army had advanced ten miles into the Beihan area capturing Sawdanniya and Howdieh. On that day, fourteen airlifts brought two platoons of the Durham Light Infantry to picket the track from Manawa to Beihan. On this track 120 Levies were fired on during January 13 and two days later, some Yemenis occupied some sixty to seventy square miles of Protectorate territory in the Beihan area. These occupying forces ignored several requests from the Aden Government to withdraw, with the consequence that RAF jet aircraft attacked Sawdanniya and Howdieh and expelled them. Dhala airfield was attacked on January 27; the Levies pursued the tribesmen but were engaged by a large force of Yemeni troops and tribesmen, and it was not until the Cameron Highlanders were brought into action that the Yemenis were driven back across the frontier with the loss of thirty lives. A patrol of Cameron Highlanders was ambushed near Dhala on February 4 with the loss of two killed and six wounded. The attackers had come from Danaba; this village was bombed and destroyed by the RAF as a reprisal seven days later, after warnings to the inhabitants to evacuate.

In the meantime, Tawfik Chamandy, the Yemeni Delegate to the United Nations, announced in the Trusteeship Council that Aden was an 'integral part of Yemen.' On January 22, Great Britain, in reply, distributed a Memorandum within the Security Council stating that the Yemen had stirred up the frontier tribes in the Aden Protectorate over a period of years. Later, on February 16, another Memorandum referred to firm evidence in British hands proving that Egypt and Communist countries were supplying military assistance to the Yemen; it further mentioned that Egyptian Army instructors were training the Yemeni Army.

On December 4, 1956, the Yemeni Government proposed a meeting to settle the frontier dispute, but for four weeks no reply could be obtained from them to a request for more detailed proposals. In mid-January 1957, the Foreign Office had no knowledge of an official proposal to demarcate the frontier by means of an International Commission. However, it later announced that an attempt was being made to arrange a border meeting between Aden and Yemen representatives with a view to ending the fighting. The Foreign Office were negotiating with Seiyid Hasan Ibrahim, Yemeni Chargé d'Affaires in London, and Sir William Luce, Governor of Aden, was consulting the rulers of the Protectorate territories concerned. The rulers agreed that the frontier meeting should take place, but the Sherif of Beihan insisted that Yemeni troops and tribesmen should first evacuate their positions overlooking his village of Shaghir.

The British Government announced on January 17 that they would be prepared for discussions to take place at the frontier customs post at Sana subject to the demands of the Sherif of Beihan that Yemenis should evacuate his territory and that they should restore his customary use of the water source at Husein Faqih from which Naqd Marqad a frontier village on the Beihan-Yemen border, draws its supply.

The reply of the Yemeni Government on January 22 inferred that it would discuss nothing but its claim to the whole of the Aden Protectorate. This was quite unacceptable to the British Government. However, by February 12, all Yemeni forces had withdrawn from Aden territory and Mr. Selwyn Lloyd sent a note on that date to the Yemeni Chargé d'Affaires in London agreeing that frontier talks should take place at Mukeiras and not at Sana on February 23. An unsatisfactory reply was received on February 27; Naqd Meizar in Beihan was attacked on February 21 and March 8 and Sana was raided on March 5, but soon afterwards this spell of unusually heavy skirmishing along the frontier died down and life temporarily resumed its normal pattern.

(vi) RUSSIANS IN THE YEMEN 1923–57

A spate of Yemeni military exuberance in 1957 was prompted by the arrival of the Russian arms at Salif in November 1956. The British did not appreciate at that time that Russian involvement in the Red Sea dated back almost thirty-five years, providing them with a wealth of local experience.

The early rulers of the Soviet Union sought to disseminate Communism from Moscow to as many diplomatic capitals as were within its reach. The fact that many of their missions were destined to eke out a monotonous existence at consulates in apparently unimportant oriental backwaters did not deter either the missions or those who sent them. One such new creation was the Russian consulate-general at Jedda, established in 1923 and nominally headed by Karim Hakimoff, who, in his younger days,

E

had been a locksmith; at the time of his appointment, he dropped his second name and took the aristocratic title of *khan*. However, the real chief of the consulate-general was the first secretary, Naoum Belkin. Only one of Hakimoff's officers was a true Russian, but the unit had the advantage of being composed entirely of men of the Muslim faith. When the Wahabis overran Jedda (in Ibn Saud's territorial expansion from the east to form what is now Saudi Arabia) the members of the mission took refuge in Eritrea and, during its short stay in the Italian colony, collected some useful information about the Yemen. Soon after its recall to Jedda by Ibn Saud, it established relations with the Imam at Sana. Hakimoff went to Sana at the head of an imposing embassy which embodied, among others, commercial aviation and medical experts. The success of this embassy was due to the zeal of Astakhoff, previously senior First Secretary of the Russian Embassy in Tokyo.

The line of Russian policy was one now familiar: a treaty of friendship, the establishment of an overstaffed consulate, trading agreements, resident doctors who have apparently legitimate reasons for getting among the people, and the dumping of surplus merchandise, creating great financial indebtedness of the country concerned to Russia. This was the primitive equivalent of economic penetration and technical assistance. Russia had taken the lead in officially recognising Ibn Saud's régime in the Hejaz in 1926 and in the following year a Russian ship duly arrived at Jedda loaded with materials for exploitation on the Hejaz markets at knock-down prices. Two years later she was first in the field to raise the status of her consulate-general in Jedda to that of legation – with Hakimoff as its first minister; however the dumping of cheap Russian goods soon became so unpopular in the Hejaz that it became necessary for the legation at Jedda to close. Then, in the nick of time, an economic crisis in both Hejaz and Nejd gave the legation a new lease of life. A Russian offer of cheap products on long-term credit was too tempting to resist, and Jedda once more came to welcome Russian shipping to her roads.

In the Yemen, events followed a similar course, temporarily with more success. At Sana, Astakhoff negotiated with Ragheb Bey a ten-year treaty of commerce and friendship which was signed on November 1, 1928. Under its provisions the Yemen was recognised as an independent kingdom and a Russian representative was to reside permanently in Sana. The treaty was ratified in Moscow on January 28, 1929, and was extended for another ten years in 1938 after correspondence between Litvinoff and the Imam. One article in the 1928 treaty laid down that, if any other country appointed a permanent representative in Sana, the Soviet government would have the right to do the same. Soon after the treaty was signed, the Russian government flooded the Yemen market with its Napthexport petroleum products, and organised permanent exhibits of agricultural implements at Hodeida and Sana. In addition large quantities of grain, sugar, starch and soap were exported to the Yemen. From 1930 onwards, two Russians were stationed in Hodeida to supervise a sample store containing lumber, cloth, toilet articles and footwear. Their trade was not brisk. In Sana the Soviet aid mission consisted of two doctors, a dentist, an engineer, and a government commercial agent. One of the staff had his wife and small son with him in Sana and one of the doctors was a woman, Fany Jaskolko. At first, things went well but, as the years went by, declining interest and lethargy on the part of the staff, besides obstruction at the hands of the Imam, resulted in stalemate. Consequently, in 1938, the whole Russian mission in the Yemen was recalled to Moscow to account for its failure – and for its private financial transactions. Those recalled, including the women, were put to death shortly afterwards. Two of them, Ali Fatahoff and Steponkoff, returned to Jedda to take refuge in Islam, but when Hakimoff embarked on September 11, 1938, it was to meet his executioners.

Such was the extent, up to 1939, of Russia's attempt to counter Italian influence on the eastern seaboard of the Red Sea. Before she could muster and re-deploy her diplomatic forces, however the war had intervened, Italy had disappeared from East Africa and most of the Italian agents were eventually removed from the Yemen at British behest. Russian activity was desultory until, in May 1944, the seeds of the Free Yemeni Party (see page 78) were sown. From that time Russian involvement in the Yemen increased many times over. Operating mainly from Aden the Party issued forth a torrent of propaganda against the Imam's rule, and in 1948 arranged his assassination. The Beihan incident of 1949, a more than ordinary frontier violation, prompted the Anglo-Yemeni agreement of 1950 – a document which, in the event, became of little practical consequence.

During the next six years the intensity of frontier incidents increased, and in August and September 1956, as we have seen, Cairo Radio carried out a full scale onslaught against Aden in an attempt to stir up an insurrection. This developed into the propaganda war of 1957 between Great Britain and the Yemen. In the meantime the Russians had been busy in Cairo. Their first move to re-establish some formal link with the Yemen came in October 1955 when Daniel Solod, Soviet Ambassador to Egypt, met the acting Yemeni Foreign Minister in Cairo. At that time they reached agreement for a renewal of the 1928 treaty, the establishment of formal diplomatic relations and the exchange of representatives. The cold war had now finally reached the Straits of Bab el-Mandeb. Russia's old motives of keeping up with the Italians were now replaced by those of harassing one of the last surviving areas of British influence in the Middle East, a strategic point where a considerable amount of Britain's overseas military strength was to be concentrated. No time was lost therefore in putting the agreement into effect. A new Russo-Yemeni treaty was signed in Cairo on November 1, 1955, and this was followed in the following March by a trade agreement, under the terms of which Russia agreed to supply 'machinery', oil products, wheat and rice in exchange for Yemeni hides, coffee and other commodities. The 'exchange' involved was largely a polite fiction.

The 'machinery' of the 1956 treaty, although not publicly specified, was to include a wide range of armaments. Gun-running into the Yemen had proved profitable ever since the 1930s when Henry de Monfreid and his German and Italian counterparts were actively engaged in that romantic profession. Although the French took some part in selling arms to the Imam, the Germans were certainly much more active and enterprising. Before the First World War the Yemeni tribes were mainly using Mausers made in 1874; these were single loaders of ·40 bore firing black powder and sighted to 1,200 metres. In 1922, the French 'geological' expedition under Vincent Cherruau offered to sell arms and ammunition to the Imam. Skoda batteries were in use in the country in 1928, and some ten years later a consignment of rifles arrived from the Skoda works. In 1934 Heinrich Hansen and another German from a Hamburg armaments firm carried through a deal with the Imam, and in that year also a Turk, Dr. Zaki Kiram, was sent to the Imam by the Germans to sell him small arms. Dr. Kiram visited the Yemen in 1936 for the same purpose.

Ibrahim Depui, representing the Fabrique Nationale, Liége, spent much time in Sana between the two world wars, trading in arms and ammunition. In 1937 Germany sold 50,000 rifles to the Imam in return for gold; the Polish Government had already rejected the rifles as faulty. These old weapons, spanning some eighty years, were still to be seen as late as 1957. At Qataba, in January of that year, Yemeni troops were using 1914 machine guns, recent Russian rifles, British rifles of various dates and Canadian, Hungarian, German, Italian and American arms made between 1900 and 1918. Lee-Enfields, Steyrs and Mannlichers were a common sight. In the same month, January 1957, a Russian-sponsored delegation of eight assembled in Cairo, with a view to further equipping the Yemeni forces with Russian armaments, and later joined a party of Russian doctors already in Taizz. The delegation arrived there by air from Jedda and was still touring the kingdom by air in early February.

All this was but a small contribution to the high incidence of foreign activity in the Yemen during 1956–7. The German mining firm, Deilman Bergbau, which was prospecting for oil in the south and coastal areas, became involved in various disputes with the so-called Yemen Development Corporation of Washington of the financier Gabler, which was similarly prospecting in the north-east. Aramco prospectors were operating in the Beihan area and Petroleum Concessions Ltd., were supposed to have found oil at Thamud and at Beihan. French experts were planning roads, and the Société des Constructions des Batignolles of Paris were busy rebuilding parts of the port of Mocha. François Balsan, the French writer-traveller, spent five exasperating months in the Yemen in 1957 dealing with the affairs of the Société, but at the same time engaged privately in archaeological work. His book *Inquiétant Yémen*, resulted from this experience.

Following the Russo-Yemeni trade agreement of March 1956, Seif al-Islam Muhamad al-Badr, the Imam's son, visited East Germany, Czechoslovakia and Moscow in June of that year. During this time the Crown Prince made arrangements for large shipments of arms to his country in return for deferred cash payments over a period of years. The Russian Government was also prepared to finance certain economic projects, unspecified at that time. Al-Badr arranged for concessions to be granted to Russia for oil prospecting and for uranium extraction, the latter on the basis of a report submitted to him by an East European 'party of specialists'.

On August 21, 1956, the Yemen formally recognised Communist China, and agreement was reached that diplomatic relations at ministerial level should be established. The next month, the Imam accepted an offer of the Czechoslovak Government to train, for six months without charge, a number of Yemenis in engineering and medicine at universities in Czechoslovakia.

(vii) YEMENI MILITARY FORCES

Up to the time of Sallal's rebellion in 1962, the regular army of the Imam consisted of some 10,000 of all ranks trained by Iraqi, and later Egyptian officers. There was also about the same number of irregulars upon which the Imam could count for support. An emergency defence force of sorts, which could be called to the colours at need, numbered possibly 50,000. There was no Yemeni air force, but there were about a dozen miscellaneous civilian-type aircraft under the Imam's control. At different times British, Swedish, Czechoslovak and Yugoslav pilots had been employed to fly them.

Progress in aviation has been slow. Following the treaty of 1926 with Italy, the Italians sent aeroplanes to Sana; however, for many years afterwards, as has already been related, flying was forbidden by the Imam after a member of his household had died in an aircraft accident. After 1946, however, the Yemeni Government purchased aircraft from Egypt and Sweden, and used pilots from those countries to train the Yemeni aircrews. Very gradually the Imam came to appreciate the potential of civil and military aviation: landing grounds at Sana, Hodeida and Taizz were improved, the old landing ground at Sana south of the town was replaced by an improved one to the north, and Imam Ahmad decided to 'modernise' the landing ground at Taizz and to equip it with a modern radio station and workshop for aircraft maintenance. When Dr. Hafez Amin Bey, an Egyptian WHO consultant, visited the Khawalan area in 1951, Imam Ahmad ordered a special arifield to be constructed at Saada, and a radio station to be installed. Each flight of the Imam's aircraft had to be authorised personally by him. Before the advent of the 1956 Russian arms imports, the Yemen possessed no military aircraft except for two small American trainers given to the Imam by Ibn Saud in 1955. At one juncture all Yemeni civil aircraft were flown by American civilians lent to the Imam from Saudi Arabian Airlines; at another time the pilots were Yugoslavs. There were a number of landing grounds for them in various parts ot the territory but all, in spite of attempted improvements, were poorly equipped. The Yemeni Navy consisted of two small coastguard cutters each armed with a machine gun.

A month or so after the beginning of the civil war in 1962, the majority of 'trained' military men in the country were under the command of Colonel Sallal, the leader of the military *coup d'état* against the Imam's régime in the autumn of 1962. Officers consisted of those previously selected by Sallal for training at the Military Adademy at Sana, and those trained in Cairo and Baghdad. At that time, in addition to about 13,000 Egyptian troops and some units of the Egyptian Air Force, Sallal had only 11,000 Yemeni soldiers under command, and no air force of his own. By October 1962, thirty Russian Yak fighters had spent six years under tarpaulins and were never used. The one Yemeni pilot who did qualify failed to continue his career.

(viii) RUSSIAN ARMS, 1956

At the end of November 1956, fifty small anti-aircraft guns from Czechoslovakia were landed at Salif from the Russian ship, *Shmela*, along with small arms, ammunition and other military equipment. The rumour that jet fighter aircraft were disembarked from this freighter was soon discounted. Egyptian instructors, who had come from the Gaza area, were sent to the Yemen to set up training centres near Sana and Hodeida and there to train the Yemeni regular army in the use of these newly arrived weapons. The *Shmela's* cargo was the subject of considerable interest in the British parliament where non-committal replies were given by the Foreign Secretary to those questioning him on the subject. However, they prompted Sir Pierson Dixon to convey to the UN Security Council on February 16, 1957, that although his government could not but be perturbed at the state of affairs he did not wish his international colleagues to take any action. The United States Government refrained from commenting publicly on these arms shipments. About June 13, 1957, a second consignment arrived at Salif and by July 12 a third and fourth shipment were being off-loaded. With these shipments, which included some multi-rocket weapons of unusual design, three types of tanks and some hundreds of tons of ammunition, arrived thirty-five smartly turned out Russian Army instructors. A further two shiploads arrived at the end of the first week of August, making six since November 1956. More small arms, anti-aircraft guns, T-34 tanks, personnel carriers and ground attack aircraft were disembarked. Spectators at Salif watched Egyptian officers supervising the off-loading, and learned from them that the Egyptians would only be concerned in showing Yemenis how to install and assemble the weapons. Russian instructors were already making their arrangements to start training the Yemeni regular army in their use. The seventh arms cargo arrived at Salif a week later. With it was a mixed band of fifty technicians – of mixed skills and several Eastern European nationalities. Among them were a number of pilots, who replaced the Swedish ones employed by the Imam to fly the aircraft of the so-called Yemeni Airline. During the fourth week in August an eighth consignment of arms arrived at Salif; the total value of this and the seven previous cargoes was about £5,000,000 sterling. The contents of this last ship brought the grand total to 30 T-34 tanks, 50 SU-100 self-propelled guns, 20 aircraft, 70 armoured troop carriers, 100 pieces of field artillery, and 100 anti-aircraft guns, and in addition various small arms and ammunition.

There was little reaction to these shipments in London. Their presence on Yemeni soil, although treated with disdain in Aden, undoubtedly increased Russian prestige in the eyes of the Yemeni Government; however, there was an uncomfortable aspect for the Yemenis, for unless Russian or Russian-sponsored mercenaries could have been employed in the Yemeni army to operate the weapons, they would have had little or no effect when used and, unless used at that time, would quickly have become unserviceable. The tanks and artillery supplied by Russia were in fact obsolete by Western standards and would have required a first-class, experienced armoured regiment, trained to British or Russian standards, to operate them in the Yemen–Aden border country; also, their value in the frontier hills against well-deployed infantry would have been negligible. It now became obvious that the

Russians had taken full advantage of the well-known naïvety of Muhamad al-Badr during his visit to Moscow in June 1956. The lavish entertainment provided for the Crown Prince only resulted in his running the Yemen into debt to the tune of some five million pounds, in exchange for a large amount of obsolete military equipment which his own troops could not operate or maintain. The Imam placed many of these arms permanently in store alongside those supplied by the Germans before the Second World War. This action may have been partly due to his reluctance to create a substantial military force which could have been employed by his sons or brothers to usurp the throne. Perhaps the most interesting aspect of the shipments was the extent not so much of Russian, but of Egyptian participation. There was good reason for this.

Egypt and the Yemen signed a Treaty of Friendship in May 1947 and exchanged their first diplomatic representatives four years later. A year or so after the treaty was signed, the new Imam Ahmad was becoming increasingly worried about British 'expansionist' activities in the Aden protectorates. At this time Great Britain was beginning to implement her policy of developing the resources, administration and population of the Aden hinterland, whose chiefs had long-standing treaties of protection with the British Government. British proposals for a federation of these protected territories, first made known in January 1954, increased the Imam's anxiety, and at the end of 1955, just when the most recent of his many attempts to arrange for the development of various natural resources had come to nought, he turned in desperation to Egypt. Nasser was glad to have the Imam in his web and to exploit to the full Yemeni-British disagreement on the interpretation of the *status quo* clause in the 1934 Treaty of Sana. In April 1956 Imam Ahmad met Nasser and King Saud at Jedda and signed the Jedda Pact. This gave Egypt its formal entrée into the Yemen, and in March 1958 Nasser extended his influence there by the incorporation of the Yemen into the United Arab Republic. At the end of 1961 Syria broke away from the UAR, and the Imam also soon opted out of this loose confederation of incompatibles. But it was too late. By 1959 Egyptian officers in the Yemen had already singled out the 37-year-old Yemeni blacksmith's son, Colonel Sallal, and were laying plans for him which were to come to fruition in September 1962.

F

The first ten years of Russo-Yemeni relations ended in disaster for the Russians, and in failure to reduce Italian influence in the Red Sea. After the war, British hegemony in the eastern Mediterranean survived barely ten years of dogged political rearguard action carried on by an impoverished Whitehall. When it was clear to Russia that the tide had finally turned, Cairo became the focal point of a new Russian diplomatic *putsch* in the Middle East.

The Yemen was an obvious base from which to embarrass the British. But there were problems. The country had been supplied with small arms over a period of years but its military and economic potential was practically non-existent. Consequently the provision of 'technical assistance' was resorted to from 1955 onward amid some international competition. Closely linked with these measures were the comparatively large shipments of arms to the Yemen in 1956 and 1957. But it is hardly conceivable that Seif al-Islam al-Badr, in arranging the deal, could have believed that his own military resources would be able to put the armaments to good account. It is even more remarkable that Nasser and Khrushchev did not come earlier to realise the incongruities of the situation, because, notwithstanding the usual provocation of frontier incidents, it took them until the end of 1962 to put Sallal into action, and until later still to send him substantial reinforcements. As events have shown, the Cairo–Moscow axis made a serious misjudgement. Instead of being able to unite the Yemen's military strength, such as it was, with that of Egypt and set it on the road towards the south-west, all its attention had been turned inwards with the aim of establishing itself for its first effective thrust against the British in South-west Arabia. The rectification of this setback is only a matter of time.

7

ROYALIST VERSUS REPUBLICAN YEMEN

(i) BEIHAN AGAIN 1957

The frontier incidents which took place in the latter half of 1957 were not accompanied by a propaganda campaign as vehement as the one which had been mounted during the first three months of the year. Trouble broke out again after a lull of some three months, and continued intermittently, with a further series of protests by the Yemeni Government to the Foreign Office in London.

The Beihan area once again became the centre of Yemeni incursions. By June 1957 a considerable number of Yemeni troops and tribesmen had established themselves in Beihan territory; they fired on RAF aircraft with anti-aircraft guns, and a protest was handed to the Yemeni Chargé d'Affaires in London. The protest note asked that Yemeni regular forces and tribesmen be withdrawn immediately and that the strictest instructions be issued to the effect that RAF aircraft were not to be fired upon. No reply was received, but at the end of June the Yemeni Legation in London alleged that Great Britain had made an unprovoked attack on the Harib area and this was the cause of the incident in mid June. Two more protests were made in July by the Legation against the actions of British forces in the Harib area, and in the meanwhile Yemeni forces crossed the frontier from Harib to occupy high ground at Shuqair thus denying to the Aden forces this vantage point from which troop movements in the Harib area could be observed. There were two other Yemeni protests in early August against 'savage attacks by the British', and on August 8, Abu Taleb, the Yemeni Minister in Cairo, raised the question of these attacks in the Political Committee of the Arab League, relating them closely to the 'armed attack on Oman'. In Aden it was stated officially that the RAF would continue to attack Yemeni troops who took up illegal positions in the Western Aden Protectorate and that, so long as the Yemeni Government continued to allow their forces to occupy Protectorate territory, they must expect those forces to be attacked by the Aden security forces.

The Aden Government was fully aware that Yemeni troops and armament were being built up in Harib, and that the Yemeni Government did not wish this movement to be observed from the high ground in Beihan territory, opposite Harib.

Yet another protest against the incidents of early August was delivered to the head of the Foreign Office's Eastern Department, by Hasan Ibrahim but the Note was handed back unopened. However, Yemeni forces continued to occupy the hills near Beihan and the Protectorate forces still attempted to dislodge them. A further threat now issued from Abu Taleb in Cairo to the affect that the 'continued British aggressive acts would turn the present war into a major war'. Seiyid Hasan Ibrahim called at the Foreign Office towards the end of August to protest against more attacks on the Yemen, and a long statement was issued by the Yemeni Legation in London. At the end of the month another protest was delivered to the Foreign Office, this time by post, but it was returned to the Yemeni Legation. This Note referred to more attacks in the Beihan area, and implied that gas or napalm bombs were used by the RAF. The Foreign Office, however, confirmed its intention to continue to attack Shuqair until Yemeni forces evacuated the area and returned to their own territory. No napalm bombs had in fact been used, and the type dropped on this occasion had been 20-lb. fragmentation bombs, of the type used during the Second World War for anti-personnel work. There were more skirmishes in the Harib area in September, and at the beginning of October the Yemenis turned their attention to the Dhala area, when at the beginning of October an Aden Government Guard was killed and two were wounded in a skirmish near the village of Al-Hussein. The last in the current series of protests raised by the Yemeni Chargé d'Affaires in London alleged that RAF aircraft were still overflying the border. Fighting continued near Mukeiras until the end of October.

(ii) LONDON TALKS 1957

A former chairman of the United States Foreign Affairs Committee, James P. Richards, visited Sana in April 1957, and had audiences with the Imam and the Crown Prince. The object of the visit was to explain the Eisenhower Doctrine to the Yemeni Government, but the Americans had little success and the standard diplomatic platitudes were resorted to at the end of the session. 'The talks', they said, 'were friendly in spirit, resulting in increased understanding of President Eisenhower's policy' and it was hoped that they had 'promoted relations between the two countries'. Five months later, at the beginning of September 1957, an American economic mission representing the State Department and the International Co-operation Administration went to the Yemen at the invitation of the Imam. As it stated itself, the Mission was unconnected with the Eisenhower Doctrine. It stayed about a month and carried out an economic survey with special reference to agriculture, road building and airfield construction with the object of determining the most suitable type of aid which the USA could provide. It was not an arms mission and there was no question of American military aid being given.

In spite of these friendly overtures by the United States, Seif al-Islam Muhamad al-Badr, when stopping the night in Cairo on November 9 after talks with Colonel Nasser, said that his country had definitely rejected the Eisenhower Doctrine. On this occasion, the Crown Prince and his entourage were on their way to London where they had been invited to stay as the guests of the British Government. 'The only aim of our visit to London', the Prince said in Cairo, 'is to achieve the complete evacuation of British troops from the southern Yemen. The London visit does not mean an alteration of the Yemen's international orientation. . . . . We are Russia's friends and we will respond to an invitation to visit People's China. My London visit has one aim, which is to extricate the Yemen Protectorates from the clutch of British protection. . . . We will accept nothing but the evacuation of British troops as a solution. If we are not successful in our mission, we know our way.' However, Al-Badr duly arrived at London Airport on the evening of November 10, and on landing said that he was confident that his talks with representatives of the British Government and leaders of public opinion in Britain were going to create an atmosphere favourable for the achievement of the purposes of both sides. It was high time to put an end to outstanding disputes and to terminate the state of unrest which had lasted for so long. 'I hope', he said, 'that this visit can start for Anglo–Yemeni relations a new era of constructive understanding and positive progress on the basis of mutual respect and appreciation of the legitimate rights of both parties. My father and his Government

appreciate the real value for both parties of sincere friendship.'
Such was the situation when, on November 11, Mr. Selwyn
Lloyd opened his talks with the Prince. On that day proposed
constitutional changes in Aden were announced which provided
for an elected majority in the Legislative Council. Four days
before this the formation of a new military command for Aden
was announced. Al-Badr had further talks at the Foreign Office in
November and he visited the Houses of Parliament. It was not
expected that the visit to London would be other than a 'goodwill'
visit or that it would produce any settlement of the frontier situation. The Yemeni delegation continued to press its claim (based
on historical precedent) to Aden Colony and the Protectorates and
Kamaran. After the talks it took the view publicly that a final
settlement of the 'territorial dispute' could now be worked out,
and that an arrangement on the frontier could now be agreed.
To the Foreign Office, however, it was obvious that the respective
governments were still too far apart in their policies for agreement
to be possible. The British Government would never concede that
the Yemeni claims to Aden were valid; but the Foreign Office
were prepared to agree to the setting up of some permanent
Anglo–Yemeni conciliation machinery, as a more practical attempt
to pacify the *de facto* frontier. This was provided for in the 1951
talks but had never been put into practice.

Seiyid Hassan Ibrahim, Deputy Foreign Minister, who had
headed the Prince's delegation of six prominent Yemenis (including Muhamad Abdullah al-Amri; Muhamad Abdullah Al-
Shami, Naib of Beidha; and Abu Taleb, Chargé d'Affaires in
London), appeared disgruntled with the outcome of the talks.
'Frankly, we are disappointed,' he said. 'All we can do now is to
hope, but our hopes of a change in Britain's attitude are not high.'

(iii) SALLAL'S COUP D'ETAT 1962

Although the London talks at the end of 1957 had ended in yet
another stalemate, and Seif al-Islam al-Badr had immediately
left for countries behind the Iron Curtain, there were signs at the
beginning of 1958 that the Yemen was prepared to take part in
further talks. However, the formation by Egypt, in February
1958, of the United Arab Republic of Egypt and Syria and the
adherence to it in March of the Yemen also, forming the United

Arab States, overshadowed any interest in such talks. The Yemen continued to stir up trouble in the Protectorates. In April there were demonstrations in the Dhala area against the British régime, and such firm military action was taken by the Aden Government that a long period of calm followed. The advent of the United Arab States and the defeat of the uprisings in the Dhala area had two effects: first, a further attempt to resolve Anglo–Yemeni problems by discussion and, secondly, a revived interest in Federation on the part of the rulers of the Western Aden Protectorate states. The Emperor of Ethiopia lent his palace at Diredawa for the Anglo–Yemeni talks which took place in July; the talks came to nothing as the Imam persisted in his claim to the whole of the Aden Protectorates. Nevertheless, because the Imam was worried about a trend towards consolidation in the Western Aden Protectorate, the frontier remained fairly quiet for the rest of the year.

The failure of the Diredawa talks and the Imam's increasingly aggressive attitude revived the interest of the rulers of the Audhali, Beihan and Fadhli Sultanates in Federation. Joined later by the Amir of Dhala and the Upper Aulaqi Sheikh, they went to London in July to press for the implementation of the Federation concept. These five were joined in turn by the Lower Yafai Sultanate, and in the middle of February the next year, in the wake of an anti-Federation campaign by the Secretary-General of the Arab League, the Federation of Arab Amirates of the South was born and a new treaty was made between the Federation and Great Britain. In December 1958 the cousin of the Sultan of Lahej, Amir Fadhl bin Ali, had been elected the new Sultan and he joined the Federation, as its seventh member, in October 1959.

Meanwhile, in April 1959, Imam Ahmad had to go to Rome for medical treatment. His son Seif al-Islam al-Badr was left in control, and the Yemen soon underwent internal upheaval. Al-Badr toured the country in an attempt to counteract Zeidi opposition to the intensification of Egyptian influence, in spite of which most of his subjects were prepared to side against the Imamate. He dismissed the Zeidi Governor of Sana, appointed Egyptians to responsible posts and ruthlessly executed a number of army officers. In Al-Badr's apparently ardent pro-Nasserism, there was a mixture of pure opportunism with a desire in this way to help the kingdom. The Imam returned from Rome towards the end of the year and regained his authority with some difficulty. There were attempts on his life in 1960 and 1961. In November 1961 after the break-up of the Egypt–Syria Confederation Seif al-Badr went to see Nasser. Ahmad had by now realised that by becoming a member of the United Arab States he had made a rod for his own back by allowing Egyptian influence to spread too far in his kingdom. Consequently he was emboldened by the rift between Egypt and Syria to denounce Nasser, and was relieved when, at the end of the year, Nasser disbanded the United Arab States.

But the Imam had obtained the worst of all worlds. Persuaded that Aden constituted a threat to his kingdom, he had thrown himself into the hands of Nasser, and this action, in the eyes of the Protectorate sultanates, constituted a real threat. Thus threatened, they quickly took up again the idea of Federation, to consolidate their position against the Imam. Three more rulers joined the Federation in 1960, and in April 1962 the Wahidi Sultan became the eleventh to adhere to the new constitution. Nasser, in the event, did not give help to the Imam, but proceeded to take over more and more power in the Yemen. Already in 1959 Nasser's agents had selected their man, a Zeidi colonel in the army, to lead the revolution against the Imam. While there were yet only ten states in the Federation, discussions had begun in December 1960 on the question of a merger between Aden Colony and the Federation. These discussions continued in London and Aden during 1961 and early 1962, parallel with those concerned with the reform of the Colony's constitution.

Seif al-Islam al-Badr made a vain attempt in February 1962 to resuscitate the United Arab States and to come to terms with Nasser. But time was running out. Nasser had been taking his time to infiltrate into the Yemen and his plans were laid to take the country over later in the year. After the Wahidi had joined the Federation it was renamed the Federation of South Arabia in April 1962, and a constitutional conference was held in London in July to further the Aden Colony merger project. In August agreement was reached for it to come to fruition by March 1, 1963, but, as it turned out, the merger took place in the middle of January. Further, Nasser's grip on the Yemen began to tighten and, after having made some vain attempts to rally supporters, Imam Ahmad died on September 19, 1962. Al-Badr, the new Imam, appointed Colonel Sallal as head of the army. It took

Sallal a week to manoeuvre his forces, and on September 27 he struck – carrying out a successful *coup d'état* on September 26 against the Imam's régime.

(iv) AMERICAN POLITICAL INFLUENCE

Sallal's revolution prompted the United States to take an unaccustomed interest in the affairs of South-west Arabia. American contact with the Yemen during the first forty years of the twentieth century had been slight, but after the Second World War, both on the official and unofficial levels, it was intensified.

The visit to Sana in 1945 of Harlan Clark, American Consul at Aden, and Commander Alfred Palmer, who was in charge of the US Armed Guard Dispensary at Aden, was followed by an American diplomatic mission. At the beginning of March 1946 President Truman wrote to the Imam to pave the way for the treaty which was to follow. At the same time American representatives in Cairo agreed to provide the Imam with credit of a million dollars so that he could buy equipment from the Foreign Liquidations Commission before the end of 1947. A month later Colonel William Eddy, a Syrian-born American diplomat with long experience in Arabia, went to Sana with Harlan Clark and Richard Sanger to conclude the first American treaty with the Yemen. At Sana Colonel Eddy, as head of the 'Special United States Diplomatic Mission to the Kingdom of Yemen', negotiated an agreement of Commerce and Friendship. About five weeks afterwards Seif al-Islam Abdullah rushed off to New York to discuss 'trade prospects' with the US Government, and just over a year later Yemen was admitted to the United Nations. J. Rives Childs, the US Minister at Jedda, was in the meantime appointed the first US Minister to the Yemen, presenting his credentials to the Imam at Sana on September 30, 1946. The Arabian American Oil Company was granted an oil concession, which turned out to be a useless one, in 1950 and Wendell Phillips' famous expedition to Marib in the next year was suspected of being an oil exploration party. In August 1950 Raymond Hare was appointed to succeed Childs at Jedda and the United States Naval Research Unit No. 3 (NAMRU-3) normally stationed in Cairo, under Dr. John Killough, USN, spent a lot of time in the Yemen during those years, the members of the unit going with Hare to Taizz when he

F*

presented his credentials to Imam Ahmad in July 1951. Once during this period Dr. Harry Hoogstraal, head of the Department of Medical Zoology of NAMRU-3, and three other American doctors undertook research work on tropical diseases in and around Sana. The American firm of G. E. Allen obtained an oil concession in 1954, and Gabler's erstwhile Yemen Development Corporation of Washington obtained one during the next year. By 1960 there was considerable American participation in Yemeni commercial affairs in the face of much opposition from European countries both east and west of the Iron Curtain and from Communist China.

Russia and the United Arab Republic officially recognised Sallal's régime two days after the 1962 *coup d'état*. Saudi Arabia and Jordan on the other hand aligned themselves with the Yemeni royalists, mustering under the banner of Imam Al-Badr who had narrowly escaped death on the night of the revolt. During the first week in October, Sallal's troops and aircraft were fighting on the Saudi Arabian frontier and there were several clashes between the rebels and the Imam's supporters. Sallal declared a 'Yemeni Arab Republic' and Seiyid Abd al-Rahman al-Baidani, now deputy prime minister of the rebel régime, threatened to place in jeopardy American interests in the Yemen if she did not recognise the Republic immediately. Muhsin al-Aini, the rebel Foreign Minister, also threatened to turn to the Soviet Union for help if American recognition was not forthcoming. A republican Yemen was of course not unattractive to a republican United States of America, and the latter very quickly proceeded, first to prepare the ground for its own recognition of the rebel government, and secondly to ensure that the United Nations accepted the rebels into their fold. The whole process was engineered within a period of eleven days. The first move was to see to it that the rebel voice was heard in the UN assembly: this was arranged before the end of November. After this things moved quickly. America offered to mediate between Nasser and Sallal on the one side and King Saud, King Hussein and the Imam of Yemen on the other, so that the Yemeni republic could be preserved at least in its current areas of power. In order to obtain American recognition (both Nasser and Sallal seemed to think that such recognition would help them against the British) Sallal was obliged to say, on December 18, that he would honour all treaties concluded by previous governments, including the Treaty of Sana. The following day the United States recognised the Yemeni republic. This then cleared the way for the United Nations officially to fall into line on the next day, for the British Legation at Taizz to be closed – British affairs being placed in American hands – and for America to arrange with Sallal for her work on the Mocha–Taizz road to continue under the rebel régime. Ralph Bunche, assistant UN Secretary-General, went to visit the rebels (but not the royalists), at the beginning of March 1963, and two months afterwards the UN sent Major-General Von Horn to Sana, the rebel capital, to establish a UN observer mission. A fortnight after America had brought pressure to bear on U Thant, Von Horn established his six observers in the rebel capital, but he resigned in disgust after eleven weeks of frustration. U Thant was forced to admit that the United Nations mission had failed miserably – to the extent that Egypt, far from withdrawing her troops, was in fact sending more and more down the Red Sea. At the end of the year, the United States shipped 20,000 tons of wheat into the rebel-held port of Hodeida.

In the meantime Aden Colony had acceded to the South Arabian Federation which was later joined by two more Protectorate states, bringing the total up to fourteen federated territories by April 1963. At this time Great Britain came under heavy fire at the UN for its conduct of affairs in South-west Arabia, the allegation being that the South Arabian Federation was wholly under British control and sovereignty. Great Britan made it quite clear that she would not necessarily wish to accede to guidance from the United Nations on the conduct of her colonial policy, and at the end of May she requested postponement of the departure of a UN mission which was arranging to go to Aden and study the Colony and the Federation. In the event, the Mission visited Cairo, Hodeida, Sana and Baghdad in order to obtain what evidence it could on British 'colonialism'.

'Why do the United States and the United Nations support Nasser in his war in the Yemen and recognise a régime which is transparently a Cairo puppet government?' These words were spoken to an English friend by Imam Al-Badr in his dugout in the northern Yemen early in December 1963. The Imam also pronounced upon the 'worthlessness' of the 75-strong UN disengagement mission on the Saudi–Yemen frontier. The Mission's terms of reference, devised in the previous March by the US diplomatist Ellsworth Bunker, were to interrupt arms supplies to the Yemeni royalists and ensure a withdrawal of Egyptian forces from the Yemen. The Saudis honoured their part of the agreement but by mid-December, although the Mission had been in existence for seven months, it was clear that Egypt, in spite of having agreed with the Mission to withdraw, had no intention of doing so. Indeed she had caused the delay in Dr. Bunche's visit until early March 1963 so that one of her armoured columns could take Marib. The only 'substantial' withdrawal on her part was a reduction of her troops from 30,000 to about 26,000 men about three months later. Egypt at this time was receiving considerable American aid ($270 million in 1962).

When, after eight months, on January 4, 1964, the disengagement agreement came up for review, Saudi Arabia renewed her part of it, 'in order to comply with American requirements'. The Yemeni Arab Republic openly flaunted the agreement; yet the USA continued to recognise its government. It was not clear, therefore, why the United States, the mentor of Saudi foreign policy, forbade the kingdom to assist its fellow royalists in the Yemen, and tolerated Egyptian militancy against the disengagement plan. The USA's disregard of Saudi wishes may indicate indifference to her long-term interests in Saudi oil; certainly there were signs that she was easing her grip on the oil monopoly in Saudi Arabia. The considered haste of the USA in recognising Sallal's régime in 1962 (theoretically to facilitate the eventual expulsion of Egyptian forces and to prevent a Communist take-over) was, if nothing else, miscalculated. Only the fear of inevitable resumption of Egyptian air attacks on Saudi Arabia, which would perforce have drawn Saudi-based US aircraft against the Egyptians, could have dictated the US line of denying Saudi help to the Imam. Great Britain stayed on the outside of the Yemen rebellion and kept her powder dry.

(v) EGYPTIANS AGAINST THE IMAM

The machinations of the Western powers, however, did not affect Russia's moral progress in the Yemen in the early months of 1964. By the end of 1963 Sallal's administration had already become a shadow. Major-General Anwar Qadi, the Egyptian military commander in Sana, was the real power in the land. He was succeeded in January 1964 by another Egyptian, Major-General Abd-el Mohsin Kamel Murtagi, who shortly took over from Sallal the effective leadership of the republic. This transfer of responsibility followed the mass resignation of Yemeni leaders from ministerial posts under Sallal in protest against Egyptian interference in the civil administration. The Yemeni Republicans had asked for Egyptian help but found themselves becoming puppets. Egyptian hostility to them was now further aggravated by the tightening of the Russian grip on the Egyptians. Well over 1,000 Soviet technicians were in the Yemen. About thirty Russian army officers were training republican troops in a military college at Sana; Russians were training Yemeni pilots, and were in charge of the main republican ammunition factories and depots.

In March 1964, Major-General Hamud al-Jaifi took over as Prime Minister of the Republican régime, and in the same month Sallal went to Moscow to make a treaty with Khrushchev. Afterwards he visited Czechoslovakia and Bulgaria. The British Foreign Secretary asked the US Secretary of State, Dean Rusk, whether he could not use American influence to prevent Nasser pushing the British at Aden into the sea. Both this request and the plea for the reduction of American aid to Egypt fell on stony ground. Consequently a week later British reinforcements were sent into Aden, with the result that the UN again became perturbed about 'colonialism'. Sallal flew off to Rumania in May and to China at the beginning of June. At the end of the month Nasser himself suddenly appeared in Sana and set about divesting Sallal of much of his remaining influence.

While truce talks were being held at the old Sudan Government rest house at Erkowit in the eastern Sudan, the Imam and Sallal themselves arranged a cease-fire, and a Yemeni National Reconciliation Council was planned. The aims of this council were the working out of a coalition régime for the Yemen, the exile of Sallal and Imam Al-Badr, and the retention of the Republic on more democratic lines. But there were two questions of importance, among others, which remained unresolved. One was that of the withdrawal of the 40,000 Egyptian troops, which most Yemenis of both Royalist and Republican persuasions strongly urged; the other was the sum of money which Imam Al-Badr would accept for his enforced exile. The Council, some 190 strong, was due to meet in the Northern Yemen at Sada, Abbas or Haradh on November 23. The meeting was later postponed until mid-December, but the Council never met. Egyptian aircraft had continued to harass the Imam's troops during the cease-fire, and it was quite clear that Nasser had no intention of co-operating in a settlement of the Yemen problem.

At the end of the year, while the British Colonial Secretary was on a visit there, serious rioting occurred in Aden, instigated by the Egyptian-sponsored National Liberation Front for the Liberation of the Occupied South Yemen. This party's following in Aden, which favoured union with the Yemen, was the only effective opposition to the People's Socialist Party, led by Abdullah Ansag of the Aden Trades Union Congress. Sir Kennedy Trevaskis, the High Commissioner, who had had many years of administrative experience in Aden and the Protectorates, and was closely indentified with the Federation project from its inception (indeed he had originated it), was absent from Aden on leave when the Joint Committee of Federal and Aden ministers announced that it favoured the formation of a 'unitary state' in South Arabia covering Aden, the Federation and the unfederated states. This new concept entailed a common executive, judiciary and legislature for the whole of the enlarged Federation, including Aden Colony; a transitional period would have to elapse before a common franchise and citizenship could come into force (although there does not appear to have been official support for the transitional period). If the 'unitary state' meant anything, it implied the abandonment by the Federal rulers of all their sovereignty, which would have then been sunk into the sovereignty of a single state. The conference to discuss these proposals was scheduled for March 1965; independence was promised for 1968, and it was hoped that agreement would soon be reached on the status and financial arrangements for the British military base. Meanwhile, Sir Kennedy Trevaskis, who had flown to England in October 1964 on the change of government in London, suddenly retired – at the age of 49 – and Sir Richard Turnbull, who was 55, was appointed to take his place in January 1965.

Meanwhile, once again, there had been mass resignations from Sallal's government, and by December 27, 1964, all but one of the twenty-five Cabinet members had renounced their allegiance to him. Sallal immediately left to see Nasser in Cairo, taking with him his Vice-President, Hasan al-Amri, and Abdul Hamim. A state of emergency was declared by the Egyptians early in the new year, and tribunals were set up to try the resigned Sallalist ministers, Al-Jaifi being replaced in the premiership by Hasan al-Amri, and Abdul Hamim becoming Foreign Minister. By the beginning of February, Sallal's tenure of power had become extremely insecure. It seemed only a matter of time before the Republicans themselves would be split by internal dissensions.

8

EPILOGUE 1967

(i) THE FEDERATION AND GREAT BRITAIN

At the time of Mr. Duncan Sandys' tenure of the Colonial Secretaryship, British Government policy dictated that independence should be granted to Aden and the Protectorate in 1968, that a Federation of the South Arabian states should be established and that the British military forces should continue to use the Aden base after independence, subject to a satisfactory defence agreement being signed. But by 1966 a change had come about and it was decided that a complete British withdrawal – both civil and military – from the South Arabian Federation would take place by January 1, 1968, and that the United Nations would be asked to assist the Federation during the period of transition. The aim was to leave behind an independent and stable government which would embrace all of the Federation and which would be capable of withstanding all external subversion, especially from Egypt. There was no desire to enter into a defence agreement after independence. However, at the beginning of March 1967, there were inferences that the British Government, as Mr Healy said in the House of Commons, 'plans to withdraw in 1968', and that British forces would withdraw 'after Aden had received independence'.

While Egypt was doing all in its power to thwart the arrival of the United Nations mission in Aden, U Thant was expected to announce the name of its chairman in the middle of March 1967. The mission was to arrange and supervise the implementation of the constitution of the Federation, the establishment of a caretaker government and the process of handing over the reins of power. Before the end of February the majority of the states of the Federation had agreed upon proposals for a constitution to be brought into effect after the independence which was only ten months ahead. It was hoped that these proposals would be submitted to the UN mission on its arrival in Aden. It was also likely that the mission would formulate a scheme for the organisa-

134

tion of internal security before the departure of British military forces.

The Federal government itself was beset with many problems. There was disunity and distrust within its ranks and it was opposed by Egyptian-sponsored groups and by most of the inhabitants of Aden in the press and in demonstrations. There was great difficulty in reaching agreement upon who should be the leader of the newly independent state. If terrorism continued in Aden on the unprecedented scale it had reached, it was possible that the Federation might fall completely apart. Three main political parties strove in varying degrees to embarrass the government. The moderate opposition party, the South Arabian League, had some Adeni middle-class support, although it was encouraged more from the Hadhramaut and Lahej, and received considerable assistance from Saudi Arabia. The League wanted a unified sovereign state, was against any Egyptian or Yemeni influence, and was thus a particular nuisance to Nasser. Both the Front for the Liberation of the Occupied South Yemen (FLOSY) and the banned National Liberation Front were violently opposed to the South Arabian League and to the Federal Government, although FLOSY and NLF were themselves in bitter conflict. FLOSY, the strongest of the three political groups, rejected any direction from Egypt, although most of its leaders were in exile in Egypt or the Yemen. It was necessary, therefore, for Nasser to finance and arm the NLF for the terrorist activities, over which he could then have firm control. As for the military, British troops were to remain at any rate until the end of 1967. The Federal Regular Army (formerly the Aden Protectorate Levies) was waiting in the wings – not inactively: its complement was raised to ten battalions and its training continued with the few British officers who had helped to build up the force over the past year gradually relinquishing their posts to Arab officers.

(ii) THE YEMEN AND EGYPT

Early in 1966 Nasser, due to royalist military opposition, was in grave danger of losing all that he had staked in the Yemen, but the decision of Great Britain to withdraw its forces by the end of 1967 may have spurred him into a final effort to hold on. He was pledged to supply arms to the terrorists in Aden and to eliminate the authority of the Federal government. With all his power he was attempting to undermine the Hashemite royal house in Jordan and to oppose Saudi Arabia. Those kingdoms had supported the remains of the Imam's régime in the Yemen, and a complete realignment of the Arab countries was emerging. That cornerstone of Arab unity, the struggle against Israel, was then seeming to fade away; only Syria continued the fight. Saudi Arabia shelved its dispute with Britain, as did the Sultan of Muscat and Oman over Bureimi; diplomatic relations between Great Britain and Saudi Arabia had long been re-established. Jordan, however, was able to give little help to the Royalists in the Yemen, and Saudi Arabia also was unable to help, being busy building up her own military resources, with some British contractual participation, against possible future aggression from a Republican Yemen, fired with Nasser's expansionist policy. Both Jordan and Tunisia withdrew recognition of the Republican régime in the Yemen. Nasser was convinced that Great Britain was planning some secret role for Saudi Arabia in South Arabia after independence.

In the Yemen itself, disunity reigns. The Imam, still recognised by Great Britain, but not by the USA, as the *de jure* ruler of the country, was still in control of considerable areas of the territory. The Republican Yemenis were themselves divided into those who supported Egyptian policy and the 65,000 Egyptian troops in their country, and those who were against either an Egyptian-influenced republic or a return to the Imam's régime, but in favour of a democratic republic.

By the end of 1967, great changes had come about. Sallal was finally deposed, anti-Egyptian Republican Yemeni politicians returned from captivity in Cairo to Sana and some efforts were being made by both Royalists and Republicans to come to terms. In the meantime the fighting between the NLF and FLOSY, which hastened the British military withdrawal from South Arabia, resulted in the ascendancy of the NLF, to which the South Arabian Army gave their allegiance. No NLF government was functioning in Aden when the British withdrew but British and Arab *fonctionnaires* managed to keep an administration going. It remains to be seen whether the terrorist NLF government will continue to command the respect of the majority of the South Arabian Army officers. When Aden can put its house in order it must again turn its eyes northward to assess a continuing threat from either a Republican or a Royalist Yemen.

BIBLIOGRAPHY

It is quite impossible to append an adequate bibliography of the present subject within the space of a few pages. The reader has only to turn to the following recent bibliographies on the Yemen to realise that, bibliographically, the subject is almost inexhaustable:

Eric Macro, *Bibliography on Yemen and Notes on Mocha*, Coral Gables, 1960.
Eric Macro, 'The Yemen, Some Recent Literature', *Royal Central Asian Society Journal*, Vol. 14, 1958.
M. W. Wenner, *Yemen, a Selected and Annotated Bibliography since 1960*, Library of Congress, Washington DC, 1965.

The best that can be done is to list, with occasional comment, some books and articles which serve as a useful supplement. Most of the best material is to be found in journals of learned societies, and those devoted to serious study of history and political questions. These of course are less accessible to the general reader, which is why the majority of references listed here are books.

I EARLY EUROPEAN INTEREST IN THE YEMEN

Edgar Prestage's, *The Portuguese Pioneers*, London, 1933, which has just been reprinted, is a useful general work on the subject; Sir William Foster's *England's Quest of Eastern Trade*, London, 1933, in the same series (Pioneer Histories) serves a similar purpose. The standard work on the Dutch is H. Terpstra, *De Opkomst der Westerkwartier en van de Oost-Indische Compagnie*, The Hague, 1918. Also excellent is K. Glamann, *Dutch Asiatic Trade 1620–1740*, Copenhagen, 1958.

H. Furber's *John Company at Work*, Cambridge, 1951, is a valuable research work whilst H. Weber, *La Compagnie Française des Indes*, Paris, 1904, is a standard work on early French expansion. For the Ostenders see N. Laude, *La Compagnie d'Ostende*, Brussels, 1944, and M. Huisman *La Belgique Commerciale . . . La Compagnie d'Ostende*, Brussels, 1902. For the Danes, K. Larsen, *De Dansk-Ostendische Koloniers Historie*, Copenhagen, 1907–8, and for the Swedes E. Olan, *Ostindiska Compagniets Saga*, Gothenburg, 1923. Halford Hoskins is the authority on the overland route to India, *British Routes to India*, London, 1928. Both this and J. K. Sidebottom, *The Overland Mail*, London, 1948, contain useful references.

The 1708 and 1710 Malouin voyages to Mocha are recounted in Jean de la Roque's classic, *Voyage de l'Arabie Heureuse*, Paris, 1716, and the English edition of 1732 includes Sir Henry Middleton's exploits in 1612. De la Garde-Jazier's bombardment of Mocha is described in P. F. G. Desfontaines, *Relation de l'Expedition de Moka*, Paris, 1739.

2 THE CHANGE FROM TRADE TO POLITICS

On Blankett and Popham, see C. Northcote Parkinson, *War in the Eastern Seas*, London, 1954, and Sir Home Popham, *Concise Statement of Facts* . . . , London, 1805.
The following are additional references:

Arnaud, T. J., 'Rélation d'une Voyage à Mareb . . . 1843', *Journal Asiatique*, Paris, Vol. 5, 1845.

Arnaud, T. J., 'Mission dans le Yemen', *Revue d'Egypte*, Cairo, 1885.

Botta, P. E., *Relation d'une Voyage dans l'Yémen*, Paris, 1841.

Bové, N., 'Rélation abrégée sur une Voyage Botanique . . . dans les trois Arabies', *Annales des Sciences Naturelles*, Paris, Vol. 2, 1834.

Chédufau, M., 'Géographie de l'Arabie', *Bulletin de la Societe de Geographie*, Paris, Vol. 19, 1843.

Combes, E., *Voyage en Abyssinie*, Paris, 1838

Deflers, A., *Voyage au Yémen*, Paris, 1889

Ferrett, P. V. and Galinier, J. G., *Voyage en Abyssinie*, Paris, 1847

Fontanier, V., *Narrative of a Mission to India*, 1844

Fresnel, F., 'L'Arabie vue en 1837-8', *Journal Asiatique*, Paris, Vol. 17, 1871

Guillain, M., *Documents sue l'Histoire* . . . *de Madagascar*, Paris, 1856

Halévy, J., 'Rapport sur une Mission archéologique dans le Yemen', *Journal Asiatique*, Paris, Vol. 19, 1872.

Krapf, J. L., *Travels, Researches and Missionary Labours*, London, 1860

Lefébvre, T., *Voyage en Abyssinie*, Paris, 1845–54

Noé, Comte de, *Memoires relatifs a l'Expédition anglaise* . . . *1800*, Paris, 1826

Passama, J., 'Notice géographique sur . . . Yemen', *Bulletin de la Société de Géographie de Paris*, Vol. 19, 1872

Rochet d'Héricourt, C. E., *Voyage sur la Côte orientale de la Mer Rouge*, Paris, 1841, and *Second Voyage sur les deux rives de la Mer Rouge*, Paris, 1846

Tamisier, M., *Voyage en Arabie*, Paris, 1840

Valentia, Viscount, *Voyages and Travels* . . . , London, 1808

3 BEGINNINGS OF THE FRONTIER PROBLEM

Brémond, E., *Marins à Chameau*, Paris, 1935

Bury, G. W., *Arabia Infelix*, London 1915; *The Land of Uz*, London, 1911; *Pan Islam*, London, 1919; *Reports on Journeys to Ansab* . . . , Simla, 1901

Low, C. R., *History of the Indian Navy*, London, 1877

Macro, E., 'Leland Buxton in the Yemen, 1905', *Royal Central Asian Society Journal*, Vol. 27, 1961

Rihani, A., *Around the Coasts of Arabia*, London, 1930

Wavell, A. J. B., *A Modern Pilgrim in Mecca and a Siege in Sana*, London, 1912

4 ANGLO-YEMENI RELATIONS BETWEEN TWO WORLD WARS

Amin Rihani's *Arabian Peak and Desert*, London 1930; and H. F. Jacob's *Kings of Arabia*, London 1923, and *Perfumes of Araby* London 1915 are useful. Weiss-Sonnenburg's visit is recorded in his wife Hedwig's book *Zur verbotenen Stadt, Sana'a*, Berlin 1928. R. A. B. Hamilton's books *The Uneven Road*, London 1955, and *The Kingdom of Melchior*, London 1949, are written from personal experience of political and military work on the Aden-Yemen border. Many of the references cited below are works on Italian activity:

Ansaldi, C., *Il Yemen*, Rome, 1933
Aponte, S., *La Vita Segreta dell'Arabia Felice*, Milan, 1936
Burchardt, H., *Aus dem Jemen*, Leipzig, 1926
Manzoni, R., *Il Yemen*, Rome, 1884
Petrie, P. W. R., 'An Expedition to Taizz', *Edinburgh Medical Missionary Society Quarterly Papers*, Vol. 18, No. 7, Edinburgh, 1932
Rava, M., *Nel cuore dell'Arabia Felice*, Rome, 1927
'Robertson, W.', (P. W. R. Petrie), 'Yemen Journey I and II', *Scottish Geographical Magazine*, Vol. 59, No. 2, 1943; Vol. 61, No. 2, 1945
Rossi, G. B., *Il Yemen*, Turin, 1927
Rossi, E., 'Appunti di un Viaggio nel Yemen', *Bolletino Società Geografica Italiana*, Rome, Vol. 2, Feb.–Mar. 1937
Scott, H., *In the High Yemen*, London, 1942
Symes, S., *Tour of Duty*, London, 1947
Volta, S., *La Corte de Re Yahya*, Milan, 1941
Zoli, C., 'Il Confine tra Arabia Saudita e Yemen', *Bolletino Società Geografica* Italiana, Rome, Vol. 1, Feb. 1936

The Hodeida–Sana railway project is told at first hand by Robert Deutsch in *Der Yemen*, Vienna, 1914 and 'In the Unknown Yemen', *Seagoer Magazine* Vol. 4, No. 2, London 1937; and by A. J. Beneyton in 'Railway Surveys in the Yemen', *Geographical Journal*, London, Vol. 43 No. 1, January 1914; 'Trois Années en Arabie Heureuse', *Bulletin de la Société de Géographie*, Paris, Vol. 27, No. 6, 1913, and Mission d'Etudes au Yémen, *La Géographie*, Paris, Vol. 28, No. 4, October 1913. The following should also be noted:

Barthoux, J., 'Aux Portes de Saba la mystérieuse', *Tijdskrift van het Koninklijke Nederlandsch Aardijksjundig Genootschap*, Leiden, Vol. 56, 1939
Ingrams, H., *Arabia and the Isles*, London and New York, 1966.
Lamare, P., 'Une Exploration française au Yemen', *La Nature*, No. 2844, 1 November 1930
Meulen, D. van der, *Faces in Shem*, London, 1961; *Aden to the Hadhramaut*, London, 1947; *The Wells of Ibn Saud*, London, 1957
Montagne, R., 'Au coeur de l'Arabie Heureuse', *L'illustration*, Paris, Vol. 88, Part 2, June 14, 1930
Stark, Freya, *East is West*, London 1945

5 A CHANGE OF KING

Barer, S., *The Magic Carpet*, London, 1952
Heyworth-Dunne, J., *Al-Yemen*, Cairo, 1952
Langer, S., 'Meine Reise nach Sana', *Ausland*, Vol. 55, Stuttgart, 1882
Saphir, E., *Eben Saphir*, Vol. 1, Lyck, 1866; Vol. 2, Mainz, 1874
Stern, H. A., *Journal of a Missionary Journey into Arabia Felix*, London, 1858
Yavneeli, S., *Travels in the Yemen 1911–12* (in Hebrew), Tel-Aviv, 1952
Zemach, J., *Une Mission de l'Alliance dans le Yemen*, Paris, 1910

6–7 THE BEGINNING OF THE END and ROYALIST VERSUS REPUBLICAN YEMEN

Only a few of the most recent books on Aden and the Yemen can be listed here.

Bailey, F., *Harry the Locust*, London, 1957
Balsan, F., *Inquiétant Yémen*, Paris, 1960
Bethmann, E. W., *Yemen on the Threshold*, Washington DC, 1960
Brinton, J. Y., *Aden and the Federation of South Arabia*, Washington DC, 1960
Coon, C. S., *Measuring Ethiopia and a Flight into Arabia*, London, 1936
Dobson, M., *South Arabian Federation*, New York, 1967
Faroughy, A., *Introducing Yemen*, New York, 1947
Fayein, C., *Une Française Médecine au Yemen*, Paris, 1955
Helfritz, H., *The Yemen: a Secret Journey*, London, 1956
Hickenbotham, T., *Aden*, London, 1958
Hoeck, E., *Doctor among the Bedouins*, London, 1962
Holden, D., *Farewell to Arabia*, London, 1966
Ingrams, H., *The Yemen*, London and New York, 1963
Johnston, C., *The View from Steamer Point*, London and New York, 1965
King, G., *Imperial Outpost, Aden*, London, 1964
Knox-Mawer, J., *The Sultans Came to Tea*, London, 1962
Lunt, J., *The Barren Rocks of Aden*, London, 1966
Pawelke, G., *Jemen, das Verbotene Land*, Düsseldorf, 1959
Phillips, W., *Qataban and Sheba*, London, 1955
Reilly, B., *Aden and the Yemen*, London, 1960
Sanger, R. H., *The Arabian Peninsula*, New York, 1954
Schmidt, D., *The Unknown War: the Yemen, Past, Present and Future*, London, 1967
Shaffer, R., *Tents and Towers of Arabia*, New York, 1952
Somerville-Large, P., *Tribes and Tribulations*, London, 1967
Twitchell, K. S., *Saudi Arabia*, Princeton, 1947
Walford, G. F., *Arabian Locust Hunter*, London, 1963
Wenner, M. W., *Modern Yemen 1918–1966*, New York, 1967
Zwemer, S., *Arabia, the Cradle of Islam*, New York, 1900

INDEX